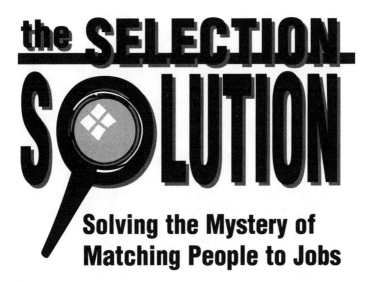

the SELECTION SOLUTION

Solving the Mystery of Matching People to Jobs

William C. Byham, Ph.D.

with Steven M. Krauzer

Published by DDI Press, c/o Development Dimensions International, World Headquarters—Pittsburgh, 1225 Washington Pike, Bridgeville, Pennsylvania 15017-2838.

Manufactured in the United States of America.

Library of Congress Cataloging-in-Publications Data:

Byham, William C.
The Selection Solution: Solving the Mystery of Matching People to Jobs
1. Communications in management. 2. Interpersonal relations
ISBN 0-9623483-3-3

---

10 9 8 7 6 5 4 3 2

Introduction
Why Should You Read This Book?

There is no greater mystery than predicting human behavior— particularly when it comes to employee selection or promotion. Decisions to bring an individual into an organization or to promote someone are among the most important decisions made by leaders, and those decisions are becoming more important and more difficult. Organizations have slimmed down, thus, making every remaining job more important to organizational success. Job responsibilities are enlarging and changing rapidly, requiring different incumbent skills. There is no time to try out a number of individuals in open positions, hoping that one will succeed.

►

Some people think accuracy in hiring decisions is just luck—"You get some good ones and some poor ones." Others see selection as an inherited art. Still others believe effective interviewing methods can be learned through the trial and error associated with conducting multiple interviews. All of these people are wrong!

Interviewing effectiveness, as measured in documented productivity improvements, decreased employee turnover, and better customer satisfaction, can be improved. Interviewing is a science, not an art. But the skills are very difficult to learn intuitively by trial and error. Too much time passes between asking questions in an interview and determining the success of the individual on the job. Most importantly, interviewers never see how good a rejected individual could have been if hired. Thus, they continue to overlook high-potential applicants.

I have always thought that making a good selection decision was very much like solving a mystery—not a mystery involving "who dunnit," but "who will do it." As in a good mystery, the detective (interviewer) must obtain facts and interpret them correctly. Interviewers and detectives sometimes make decisions by themselves. But most often they must work with others who are independently collecting evidence. Thus, both interviewers and detectives must have methods of sharing and interpreting data obtained from all sources.

It is in a well-conducted data integration session, where the interviewers share data about each candidate and make appropriate decisions, that the parallels with solving a mystery are the strongest. Many times I've seen individuals who, at first glance, seemed inappropriate for a job, but when several interviewers shared and considered the data collected, they found the individuals to be excellent candidates. At other times I've come across individuals who appeared to be ready-made for the position but who had hidden flaws or mismatched motivations. At the end of a Targeted Selection® data integration session, interviewers feel that they've solved a mystery and made the correct decision.

This book is based on the Targeted Selection interviewing system that Development Dimensions International has been developing and perfecting for 25 years. It is used successfully by more than 100 of the *Fortune* 500 companies and by more than 2,500 organizations throughout the world. More than three dozen research studies have documented its effectiveness.

Why is This Book Written as a Business Novel?

To make it easier to read and understand. Why read a boring book you might not complete with content you'll probably forget? The business novel approach, which I've used in two other books (*Zapp!*® *The Lightning of Empowerment* and *HeroZ*™*—Empower Yourself, Your Coworkers, Your Company*), makes learning enjoyable and helps the reader to understand and remember salient points.

Good luck in your short course in detective techniques. It will pay off in selecting better, happier people and an organization staffed to meet your goals.

William C. Byham, Ph.D.
President and CEO
Development Dimensions International, Inc.

CHAPTER ONE

Fred Hunt found the odd-looking
envelope near the bottom of the stack
that Bernadette, the mail-room person,
had deposited on his desk blotter a half hour
earlier. Noting the absence of a return address,
Fred slit it open and read:

remember The CHameleon? One of the candidates for your position is the same kind of professional faker if you employ him or her you will be in trouble again Think about it a friend

Fred stared at the astonishing message. Hoping to clear his head, he rose from his desk and told Susan, his secretary, that he'd return soon. Fred wandered to the elevator and punched a button.

All seemed normal at UnitedCo. Two floors above in Assembly, assemblers assembled. In Research and Development, Fred found staff members researching and developing, and up another story, accountants were accounting. And on the top level, senior managers were managing. . . . Though not all of them.

When Fred returned to the Sales Department, The Boss was standing by Fred's desk, smiling pleasantly. "The ball is in your court on hiring your new person, Fred," he said, "but I wanted to assure you that I'm available if you need any advice."

Fred decided he needed advice now. He had to hire a new central district sales representative as soon as possible.

Fred handed The Boss the anonymous letter. The Boss frowned as he read, then looked up. "What do you think we should do, Fred?" The Boss asked.

Fred came to a decision. "I'll uncover the culprit, whatever it takes—and before I make my hiring decision." Fred spoke with confidence—though he wished he actually felt that way.

"That's fine." The Boss clapped Fred on the shoulder. "I'm sure you'll get to the bottom of this mystery."

As The Boss exited, Fred noticed a copy of *The City*

News-Gazette on his desk. He didn't recall bringing it to work. . . .

It was nearly noon. Taking the newspaper and letter with him, Fred decided to go out for lunch. Some fresh air might do him good, and besides, today's special in the company cafeteria was Chef's Surprise. Fred felt he'd already had enough surprises for one day.

CHAPTER TWO

Paula Pointer was finishing a lettuce, tomato, and yogurt dressing sandwich on multigrain bread when Jimmy Swift entered the office. "Congratulate me," he said. "I just cracked The Magillicuddy Caper."

"Congratulations," Paula said dryly. "Who did it?"

"Sven Svensen, the night security guard," Jimmy announced. "I gave him the third degree."

Paula sighed. A few days earlier, the CEO of Magillicuddy Industries had hired Paula to solve the mystery of the disappearance of some sales reports. The CEO suspected industrial espionage.

"I spoke to Mr. Svensen too," Paula said. "He told me that he felt indebted to the company for his job. He'd had some difficulty finding employment because English is his second language, and he doesn't read or write in it."

"I don't care if he . . . huh?" Jimmy drew up short. "If he couldn't read, he wouldn't know which documents to steal." Jimmy looked glum. "I suppose you know who the culprit is." Paula usually did.

She nodded. "Interviewing the CEO, I learned that he received the sales reports each Wednesday—at the same time he acquired weekly results for the company softball team, the Magillicuddy Seals."

"What's that got to do with it?" Jimmy demanded.

"In the file for the sales reports, we found three sets of box scores," Paula said. "The missing documents were one drawer down—in the file labeled '*Seals* Reports.' The CEO has an appointment with his optometrist first thing tomorrow, Kid."

"I guess I jumped to conclusions," Jimmy said, "and don't call me 'Kid.'"

The bell on the door to the outer office sounded. There Paula found a man in a business suit, who introduced himself as Fred Hunt, regional sales manager at UnitedCo. Paula ushered him into her inner sanctum. "Are you Paula Pointer, Private Investigator?" he asked.

Paula nodded. "And this is my associate . . ."

"James Swift," Jimmy interrupted, offering his hand. "What's your beef?"

Fred took in Jimmy's apparel: slouch hat, trench coat, and heavy wing tips. "Is Mr. Swift a detective too?" Fred asked.

"He wants to be . . . when he grows up," Paula wisecracked. "How can we help you?"

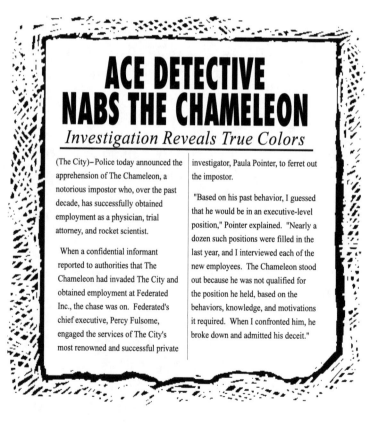

ACE DETECTIVE NABS THE CHAMELEON
Investigation Reveals True Colors

(The City)–Police today announced the apprehension of The Chameleon, a notorious impostor who, over the past decade, has successfully obtained employment as a physician, trial attorney, and rocket scientist.

When a confidential informant reported to authorities that The Chameleon had invaded The City and obtained employment at Federated Inc., the chase was on. Federated's chief executive, Percy Fulsome, engaged the services of The City's most renowned and successful private investigator, Paula Pointer, to ferret out the impostor.

"Based on his past behavior, I guessed that he would be in an executive-level position," Pointer explained. "Nearly a dozen such positions were filled in the last year, and I interviewed each of the new employees. The Chameleon stood out because he was not qualified for the position he held, based on the behaviors, knowledge, and motivations it required. When I confronted him, he broke down and admitted his deceit."

Fred told her about finding the *News-Gazette* on his desk after The Boss' visit. "I didn't notice at the time that this copy is a month old. I wonder how it found its way to my office." Fred presented the newspaper. "Never mind—it was folded to this front-page article."

"I fear that I'm facing a similar impostor," Fred said. He showed Paula the anonymous letter, and Jimmy came around to read over her shoulder.

As they perused the missive, Fred looked around Paula's office. She didn't spend much money on "front"— besides the basic furnishings, the decor was limited to a giveaway calendar from City Automotive Supply, a hat rack, and an earthenware pot containing an avocado tree.

"When The Boss called it a mystery, and by coincidence I saw that story," Fred explained, "I decided that a detective was just what I needed."

"You came to the right place," Jimmy said.

"I must warn you that this is more complex than first meets the eye," Fred said.

Paula gave him an encouraging smile. "Why don't you start at the beginning?"

CHAPTER THREE

The letter was especially distressing, Fred explained, because in his five years as regional sales manager, only about half of the persons he hired had worked out. And it had just happened again—two weeks ago the incumbent in the key position of central district sales representative, Joe Jackson, announced he was leaving to go to AcmeCorp, even though he'd done a good job for UnitedCo and seemed satisfied with the work.

"I must not make the same mistake again," Fred said. "When an employee doesn't work out, the loss to the company is substantial." Fred took a computer printout from his

```
 II Budget Worksheet

            Fiscal Year Summary COST OF A BAD HIRE
 = = = = = = = = = = = = = = = = = = = = = = = = = = =
 Description                                    Cost
 = = = = =                                    = = = = =

 ADS: 3X$1,500                        =        $4,500
 Training, 3 months salary, and benefits =     $14,000
 Interviewer cost                     =        $1,350
 Administrative cost                  =          $400
 Average candidate travel costs       =        $1,200
 Lost sales while district is uncovered =      $120,000
 Average relocation costs             =        $50,000

                                              = = = = =

 COST OF A BAD HIRE                   =        $191,450
```

briefcase. "This spreadsheet I worked up shows the typical cost of a bad hire."

"I'm afraid that time is of the essence," Fred said. "Today is Monday, and I was hoping to be able to make my job offer by no later than a week from now."

Paula was lost in thought. "We'll have a drink," she decided. From her bottom desk drawer, Paula produced three glasses and a bottle labeled "Old Overshoe Bourbon."

"It's a little early for me. No offense," Fred added quickly. "I know you private eyes enjoy your hooch.

That's the term, isn't it?"

"I'll have his," Jimmy said. "Rotgut is like mother's milk to me."

Paula half-filled each tumbler with amber liquid. Jimmy swigged his glass and gagged. "Son of a bivalve!" he swore. "That's tea!"

"Herbal, to be exact," Paula confirmed.

Fred took a tentative sip. "You can see why it's so important that the next person I select will succeed at the position," he said.

"That's not likely if you select The Faker," Jimmy said. "We've got to expose him."

"Or her," Paula corrected.

"Will you take the case?" Fred asked.

Paula nodded. "I think we can be of help," she said.

CHAPTER FOUR

"**T**he usual," Jimmy Swift said out of the side of his mouth. To Jimmy's mind, Maloney's Saloon was just the sort of place for a hard-boiled detective to hang out—a rough-and-tumble joint in The City's waterfront district, with scarred wooden furniture, a pool table with torn felt, and a black velvet painting of Elvis playing poker with bulldogs.

Maloney was a big ex-pug with a face like a boot print and a perpetual sneer. Jimmy sneered back as he placed his order, then pried himself off the bar and returned to the table, sawdust and peanut shells crunching under his wing tips.

►

Jimmy took a chair across from Paula, making sure he wasn't sitting with his back to any tough mugs, although truth to tell, most of the other customers wore business suits. The joint was jumping; the special this evening was sodium-free spring water on tap and an all-you-can-eat arugula salad bar. Maloney arrived with their drinks and said, "Isn't that trench coat kind of warm for this weather?"

Jimmy gave him a two-spot. "Don't keep the change." He stared morosely at his grapefruit juice. "I'd rather have a shot of rye with a short beer," he complained. "That was like meat and potatoes to detectives in the old days."

"These are the new days," Paula said, "and you're going to learn to be a new kind of detective if it gives me a hernia. Anyway, you don't indulge in alcoholic beverages."

"I've had my vices," Jimmy objected. "All your best detectives have a dark past."

"Oh, I wouldn't be that ashamed of having worked for Moe Bannon," Paula teased.

Moe was a colleague of Paula's who tended to take on rather unsavory cases. A month earlier, Jimmy had come to Paula and explained that he was dissatisfied with his employment under Moe. While they'd solved some mysteries, others had eluded them—and even in their successes, Jimmy sensed that lucky breaks too often played a major role.

"There's got to be a system to this private-eye game," Jimmy told Paula when she interviewed him. "And the word around The City is that you know its secrets. I want to learn them."

Paula asked Jimmy about the circumstances of cases he'd handled, how he'd attempted to solve them, and what results he'd achieved. From his replies, she learned that, despite an impetuous streak, he did have the qualifications of good judgment, an analytical bent of mind, and persistence. She felt she could build on these positive attributes, and she agreed to take him on.

Now, in the saloon, Paula saw Fred enter. They'd agreed to meet at Maloney's after Fred put together some documents on the mystery.

"I've brought you the files on my four final candidates, Paula," Fred said as he joined them. He produced folders from his briefcase. "You'll find copies of their applications, resumes, and other related material. We can discuss them in detail once you've had a chance to go over them."

A clamor arose at the bar. Jimmy turned to see that two fellows had risen from their stools and were snarling nose to nose. Maloney came around the counter, grabbed them by their collars, paused while they retrieved their attaché cases, and frog-marched them out the door.

Maloney dusted his hands as he stopped at their table. "Those guys never could handle their papaya juice," he said. "They'll feel better in the morning."

"Fighting over some dame?" Jimmy guessed.

"Actually," Maloney said, "one of them insisted that John Maynard Keynes' theory of economic equilibrium is empirically unimpeachable, while the other claimed that Adam Smith's 'invisible hand' of competition guides the system." Maloney spit on the floor. "Personally, I've always been a Keynesian."

Jimmy stared at Maloney's retreating back. "What was he talking about?"

"Business," Paula said. "Let's get back to it."

"Right," Jimmy said briskly. "Now, here's how I see it. We'll talk to the professional and personal references these candidates have provided to Fred. Whichever one gets a bad rap is The Faker."

"Actually, our organization does check references," Fred said, "although usually not until we've chosen a person for the job. We use the reference data to clarify and confirm the information we get from our interviews."

"The difficulty, Kid, is getting people to provide information that is reliable," Paula said. "You know how it is from your detective work. Nowadays people are often unwilling to open up—for fear of legal exposure."

"Or our impostor might have set up false references," Fred agreed. "Believe me, I've seen it done."

"But if someone lies on paper, they're sure to lie to your face too," Jimmy said. "This isn't getting us anywhere."

"Remember The Case of The Highway Robbery?" Paula turned to Fred. "Someone was chopping big pieces of asphalt out of Highway 6. At first, our prime suspect told Jimmy he had a bad back, but when I interviewed him, he said his favorite hobby was doing sit-ups."

"Which was pretty dumb," Jimmy snorted. "We're dealing with a more sophisticated bloke in this case. I'd bet a two-spot on it."

"You rarely get such an obvious discrepancy," Paula agreed. "But neither of us would have figured out he was dumb if we hadn't compared notes after our interviews to discover his prevarication. That's what we'll do in this case."

"I scent a whiff of your system," Jimmy commented. "How do we go about it?"

"For starters," Paula replied, "I think it best if Fred joined in this investigation."

"But that's what I'm hiring *you* for," Fred protested.

"And it could get dangerous," Jimmy said stoutly. "Felons walk these mean streets. Dames will offer a smooch and deliver an ice pick in the back. You'll get a crick in your neck from looking over your shoulder and wake up at three in the morning with the galloping heebie-jeebies. . . ."

"Kid," Paula interrupted gently, "how many times have I said that you spend too much time in the 'Mystery' section at City Books?"

"My task is discovering the top candidate for the job," Fred insisted. "Yours is discovering the top culprit for the crime."

Jimmy got back on track and saw Paula's point. "But Fred," he said, "I'm not sure we're talking about two entirely different things. In a sense, with regard to what you just said, 'job' and 'crime' are interchangeable."

"I think I understand what the Kid is saying," Paula elucidated. "You must find a candidate with the right combination of skills and motivation to be successful, while I'm searching for the person who seems qualified but isn't. In other words, my assignment is to reveal *who dunnit*. Yours is to determine *who will do it*."

"With you on the team," Jimmy said, "we'll kill two birds with one stone."

Fred considered. "I see the logic in your proposition," he agreed. "I'll do my best to be at your disposal."

Paula arranged for them to meet in the morning. As they left Maloney's, Jimmy gave Fred a reassuring pat on the back.

"Don't worry, partner," Jimmy said. "I'll take care of the rough stuff."

CHAPTER FIVE

T he next morning, Jimmy climbed into the taxi waiting in front of his boarding house. He nodded hello to Paula and demanded of the driver, "Whaddaya know about UnitedCo?"

Mack the Hack was the sort of cabbie who had the inside dope on everyone and everything. He merged into traffic. "Isn't that trench coat kind of warm for this weather?"

Paula smiled. She wore a linen dress and carried her briefcase.

"UnitedCo," Mack repeated. "Stock closed yesterday at 33 3/8, up a quarter, 26,273 shares traded. Founded 51 years ago this November, net asset value . . ."

▶

"All right, I get the idea," Jimmy interrupted. "So what's the hot tip on the third race at City Downs?"

"The smart money is on Galloping Gertie." Mack adjusted his billed cap. "She's coming off a five-win streak."

Jimmy handed Mack a two-dollar bill. "Put down a deuce for me."

Jimmy turned to Paula. "I've been thinking. On one hand you've got the fact that Fred has had a bunch of salespeople quit. On the other hand you've got The Faker."

"Sounds suspicious to me," Mack put in.

"Hey, leave the detecting to me," Jimmy admonished. To Paula he said, "How do we know that the most recent one, this Joe Jackson, wasn't paid off or persuaded to quit so this faker could get his foot in the door?"

"What do you suggest?"

"This came to me last night," Jimmy said, "and let me tell you, I had a heck of a time concentrating. The woman upstairs was practicing the rumba. One, two, three, kick! One, two, three, kick! From the screeches I heard, I think the kicks were directed at her cat."

"Try to focus, Kid," Paula said.

"Let's grill Joe Jackson and find out the real reason he's leaving."

Paula looked dubious, but before she could respond, they arrived at UnitedCo.

CHAPTER SIX

Fred's secretary, Susan, offered coffee. "Make mine black and strong," Jimmy said. Paula requested decaf with skim milk, no sugar. Joe Jackson, who was not shirking his duties during his last week on the job, was on a sales call but was scheduled to return soon.

As Susan went out, The Boss entered the office. "Hello, Paula," he said.

Fred was surprised. "You know each other?"

"Paula assisted me with a matter some years back," The Boss said. "We called it The Case of The Purloined Promotion. But never mind that. Fred, I was pleased to hear that you called

Paula in on this. With her help, I'm sure you'll solve this mystery."

The Boss turned to Paula. "I came down to arrange the terms of your service."

"Shall I dictate my standard agreement?"

"That would be fine." The Boss sat down at Fred's desk, borrowing a pen and legal pad.

"I hereby employ Paula Pointer to perform such services . . ." As Paula went on, Fred walked Jimmy to the corner of the room.

"I do appreciate your help," Fred said. "With you and Paula on the team, I know we'll put the kibosh on this charlatan."

"'The kibosh?'" Jimmy echoed incredulously.

Fred blushed. "I was using private detective lingo."

"If we're going to be partners," Jimmy growled, "you'd best leave that to me."

CHAPTER SEVEN

Joe Jackson was a forthright-appearing fellow, and his curiosity about why he had been called to Fred's office was apparent. Fred introduced Paula as his "special consultant."

Fred cleared his throat. "Joe, I wish you the best in your new position, but it would be a great help if you could explain why you're leaving us to join their sales division."

"I'm not," Joe said, to Fred's surprise. "I'll be working in-house for Customer Support."

"But you've got all the qualities of a successful sales rep," Fred protested. "When I interviewed you, I was impressed with the

◄

ways you worked with clients to resolve their complaints. You're sensitive to customers' needs, and I know that you've made yourself intimately familiar with our product line. And in fact," Fred concluded, "your sales record is satisfactory."

"I must say that 'satisfactory' is accurate, Fred," Joe mused. "You'll recall that we had several discussions on how I could meet more ambitious goals. Although I did increase my billings somewhat, I never reached the quotas we agreed on."

"I did feel that you might have been more aggressive," Fred agreed.

"That's just it," Joe said. "The reason that I know so much about UnitedCo products is that I really enjoy reading technical documentation, talking with R&D staff, and studying the mechanics of the product. And when I was in the field, I got more satisfaction in helping clients get the best use of our products than from making the actual sale."

As Fred was digesting this revelation, Jimmy came bustling in. While they'd waited for Joe, Jimmy had wandered off into the bowels of UnitedCo. "I got caught up in watching the barrow shield production line," he apologized. "It's neat how you punch those suckers out."

Jimmy gave Joe his best detective gaze. "So you're the guy who's jumping ship."

"This is my associate," Paula explained wearily.

"And don't call me 'Kid,'" Jimmy said automatically. "Now then, why are you lamming out to work in Sales at AcmeCorp?"

Joe explained again that he was giving up sales. Jimmy scoffed and told Joe that they knew he was a good rep, because Fred had told them about Joe's skills in sensitivity, problem solving, and technical knowledge. "Come on, pal, what's the real reason?" Jimmy demanded.

"I was just discussing that," Joe said, bristling slightly.

Paula rose. "Joe, thanks for your help."

"You're welcome." He shook her hand and went out.

"Now we're getting somewhere," Jimmy said.

"Perhaps," Paula said, "but don't you feel it would help if we knew where we were going?"

CHAPTER EIGHT

Riverfront Park was a block from the UnitedCo building, and the three of them adjourned there to enjoy the pleasant weather. At the kiosk near the corner, Jimmy bought a bag of birdseed with a two-spot. "Where do you get two-dollar bills these days?" Fred inquired.

"Beats me." Jimmy's mind was elsewhere. "Gee whiz, talking to Joe Jackson didn't tell me anything about whether he might have quit because The Faker bought him off."

"I think we can eliminate that idea." Fred told Jimmy what he had learned from Joe, and Jimmy noted that he'd repeated the same questions.

◄

"I'll be a boondoggled brother-sweeper!" Jimmy exclaimed when Fred's point sunk in. "Joe had all the qualifications for Customer Support, but you made him a salesman. You hired the right guy for the wrong job!" Jimmy was so caught up in his discovery that he wolfed down a handful of birdseed.

"You're dribbling birdseed on your trench coat, Kid," Paula commented.

Jimmy realized what he'd been eating and looked a bit green. A pigeon jumped on his chest, and he shooed it away.

"I'm getting an idea," Fred said. "Tell me a little more about how you solved The Case of The Chameleon."

"From the recent executive-level hires at Federated," Paula began, "I came up with four principal suspects. To learn which was the culprit, I needed to know about each of them."

"Needed to know what, exactly?" Jimmy asked.

"That's a good question," Paula replied. "Of course, we can't discover everything about a person. Even if we could, the bulk of unrelated data would become cumbersome and difficult to make sense of—and gathering it would be time-consuming. So in my system, I limit the areas where I seek information to those most relevant."

"I've tried to do that in hiring," Fred said. "I call those areas the *dimensions* of the job. Basically, it's a label for what we want to know about a person."

"I'm not sure I get it," Jimmy said.

"I try to figure out what makes people successful or unsuccessful in the different roles people play in their jobs," Fred explained. "I have a list of the dimensions of a good salesperson—although, since I haven't been doing such a good job, I don't know if the list is the problem or if it's the information I'm getting on the candidates," Fred added ruefully.

"You've got the right idea, Fred," Paula said supportively. "I've learned that what you call dimensions are essential in solving a mystery. There are three types of dimensions we need to investigate. The first and most simple is knowledge. For example, one suspect in The Case of The Chameleon was a financial officer. Clearly she'd need to know accounting, and I could check on that by seeing if she could read a balance sheet."

Fred produced a notebook from his pocket. "I hope you don't mind," he said. "I'm an inveterate note taker."

"The second is motivation," Paula continued. "In The Case of The Chameleon, I looked at the match between each suspect's motivation and the motivation opportunities offered by the job. For example, if a manager in a team-oriented organization told me she liked to work alone to figure out solutions, I would have certainly smelled a rat. The third and most important aspect, however, is behavior, and that's what ultimately led to the arrest of The Chameleon."

"But how?" Jimmy asked.

"Before I tracked him down," Paula said, "I had to learn what groups of behaviors—or as Fred terms it, behavioral dimensions—successful people in jobs like my suspects' demonstrated. The Chameleon turned out to be masquerading as marketing director. On talking to his team members and to him, it turned out he couldn't lead a meeting or coach his team members—two dimensions important in that job. Meetings took forever and produced little. Team members weren't given any help in their assignments. The organization was still functioning because sometimes the impact of behavioral dimensions are slow to show up."

"You mean his boss thought he was doing a good job?" Jimmy asked.

"Yes. The Chameleon was great at delegation. When a presentation was to be made, he just stood back and let one of his people do it. Management thought he had a part in it but was letting the team members take the credit. Actually he hadn't done anything."

"That sounds like a great way to solve this new mystery," Jimmy said. "We make sure we know the dimensions for Fred's sales position, and then we ask questions about past behaviors relative to each dimension. The Faker is a cinch bet to come up short, and then we've got our person."

"I can see now that the way I was using dimensions was somewhat lacking," Fred said. "I was too general, using things like 'gets along with people' or 'organization person.' I need to be more specific."

"Yes," said Paula, "and in my system, because several people will be using the list, you have to write out a clear definition so everyone is focusing on the same targets."

"But how do we figure out the dimensions?" Jimmy asked.

"I've got an idea on that, Jimmy," Fred said.

CHAPTER NINE

The menu in the UnitedCo company cafeteria that day included corn chowder, shepherd's pie, sloppy joes, and mystery meat. "The dietitian previously worked in a grammar school hot lunch program," Fred confided. Paula managed to find a salad at the end of the counter, and Fred led them to a table in a quiet corner where two people were already seated.

Fred introduced them as Mary Brown and Ralph Lopez, two of his top sales representatives. "I thought Mary and Ralph could tell us what they do that makes them successful," Fred explained. "After that, we can

▶

use this information to identify dimensions important for success."

A spirited discussion followed. Because Mary and Ralph also worked in Central District, they were able to offer numerous behaviors associated with success or failure in sales to the kind of customers Fred's new person would be pursuing.

By the time the long list was complete, the cafeteria was nearly empty.

Fred was in a good mood. "That was really interesting. I learned a lot myself."

"It's a good start," interjected Paula, "but we also have to learn more about what differentiates good and poor job performance. Could we meet with you and some of the other sales managers for a couple of hours?"

Three sales managers were available and agreed to meet in Fred's office to help him out. Paula started the meeting by asking each of them to think about their best salespeople and to describe differences in their knowledge, motivations, and behavior as compared to merely acceptable salespeople. It wasn't easy, but they pitched in and came up with a good list.

Next, Paula asked the same question but focused it on differences between unsuccessful salespeople and acceptable ones. Answers poured out. The sales managers told story after story about why and how people had failed. The time went fast, and at the end each of the sales managers asked for a copy of the trio's list.

After the sales managers left, Fred, Paula, and Jimmy remained in Fred's office. Sitting around a table, they organized their information into possible dimensional groupings.

Jimmy and Fred found that it was not a simple matter to categorize the knowledge, motivations, and behaviors into dimensions, and they could see that it took some training. But with Paula's detective savvy and Fred's experience as a salesperson and a manager, they made quick progress on many dimensions.

Fred kept careful track in his notebook of the dimensions critical to sales representative, including the definition of each and the key actions associated with job success.

His notebook entry looked like this:

PERSUASIVENESS/SALES ABILITY: *Using appropriate interpersonal styles and communication methods to gain acceptance of an idea, plan, activity, or product from prospects and clientele.*

- *Determine customer needs and decision criteria.*

- *Select approach appropriate to situation.*

- *Demonstrate how product or service satisfies needs.*

- *Determine nature of objections and respond appropriately.*

- *Acknowledge the customer's concerns.*

- *Gain commitment to recommended action.*

RESILIENCE: *Handling disappointment and/or rejection while maintaining effectiveness.*

- *Maintain enthusiasm after disappointment or rejection.*

- *Maintain performance after disappointment or rejection.*

- *Take criticism in stride.*

- *Bounce back quickly.*

ANALYSIS: Securing relevant information and identifying key issues and relationships from a base of information; relating and comparing data from different sources; identifying cause-effect relationships.

- Detect problems or opportunities.

- Gather all relevant information.

- Identify underlying issues or problems.

- Organize information.

- Recognize trends.

- Identify cause-effect relationships.

PLANNING AND ORGANIZING: Establishing a course of action for self and/or others to accomplish a specific goal; planning proper assignments of personnel and appropriate allocation of resources.

- Set priorities.

- Establish objectives and milestones.

- Estimate times and schedule activities.

- Identify and allocate resources.

- Use planning tools (e.g., calendar, files, charts, software, etc.).

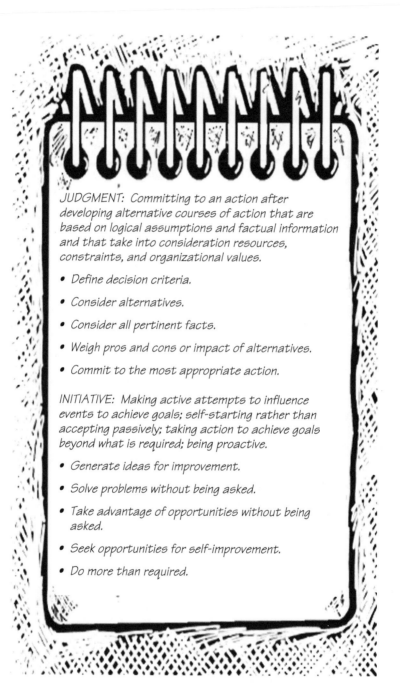

JUDGMENT: *Committing to an action after developing alternative courses of action that are based on logical assumptions and factual information and that take into consideration resources, constraints, and organizational values.*

- *Define decision criteria.*

- *Consider alternatives.*

- *Consider all pertinent facts.*

- *Weigh pros and cons or impact of alternatives.*

- *Commit to the most appropriate action.*

INITIATIVE: *Making active attempts to influence events to achieve goals; self-starting rather than accepting passively; taking action to achieve goals beyond what is required; being proactive.*

- *Generate ideas for improvement.*

- *Solve problems without being asked.*

- *Take advantage of opportunities without being asked.*

- *Seek opportunities for self-improvement.*

- *Do more than required.*

ORAL COMMUNICATION: Expressing ideas effectively in individual and group situations (including nonverbal communication); adjusting language or terminology to the characteristics and needs of the audience.

- *Mechanics—appropriate grammar and vocabulary.*
- *Organization—clear and brief.*
- *Delivery—rate, volume, gestures, eye contact.*
- *Listening.*

IMPACT: Creating a good first impression, commanding attention and respect, showing an air of confidence.

- *Speak with confident tone of voice.*
- *Maintain an attentive posture.*
- *Respond openly and warmly.*
- *Dress appropriately.*

MOTIVATIONAL FIT: The extent to which job activities and responsibilities, the organization's mode of operation and values, and the community in which the individual will live and work are consistent with the type of environment that provides personal satisfaction; the degree to which the work itself is personally satisfying.

Jimmy looked at the list with pride. "Now we know what we're aiming at," he said. "Information on the dimensions is our target, and once we hit the bull's-eye, we'll have the solutions to both unmasking the culprit and pinpointing Fred's top candidate."

Fred gave him a questioning look, but Jimmy was too taken with his discovery to notice.

"Targeted Solution!" he exclaimed. "That's what we ought to call what we're up to, because it describes your system to a T, Paula. By gaining data on the relevant dimensions of the four candidates, we target The Faker— and at the same time, Fred finds his new sales rep by targeting the dimensions important to job success!"

"By George, I think you've hit on something, Jimmy." Fred was again writing in his notebook. "I also think we've discovered the first component of our Targeted Solution system—and we've implemented it."

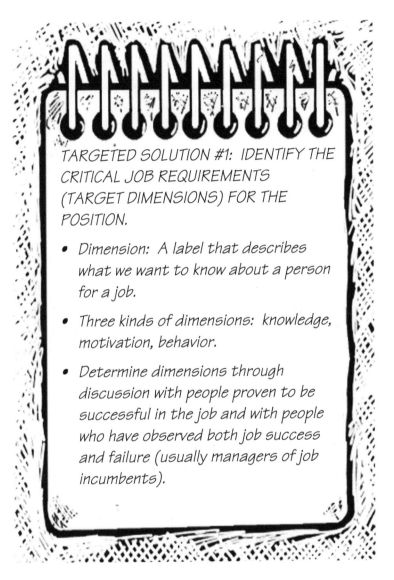

TARGETED SOLUTION #1: IDENTIFY THE CRITICAL JOB REQUIREMENTS (TARGET DIMENSIONS) FOR THE POSITION.

- *Dimension: A label that describes what we want to know about a person for a job.*

- *Three kinds of dimensions: knowledge, motivation, behavior.*

- *Determine dimensions through discussion with people proven to be successful in the job and with people who have observed both job success and failure (usually managers of job incumbents).*

Fred frowned as he studied this entry. "I understand the knowledge and behavior aspects of dimensions, but I'm not certain I grasp motivation."

"Is it like a perpetrator's choice of crimes?" Jimmy asked.

"Run with that thought, Kid," Paula encouraged.

"Say you decided to be a felon," Jimmy said. "You enjoy intricate schemes and interacting with people, but you don't like working at night and are afraid of heights. You'd probably be happier as a con artist than as a cat burglar—and if you did choose to become a cat burglar, you'd probably get caught."

"Like Joe Jackson," Fred said slowly.

"Joe Jackson is a cat burglar?" Jimmy said incredulously.

"No, but your analogy makes motivation more clear to me," Fred said. "If you like the duties of your job, you're more apt to stick with it. If not, you're more likely to be unhappy, or even leave the company—as was the case with Joe."

"But how do you figure out in advance if a person is going to like the job?" Jimmy asked.

"I think the information we got from the sales managers points us in that direction" Paula said. "They mentioned a number of activities and responsibilities that successful salespeople liked, such as independence and working with a team approach to sales. The sales managers also discussed some responsibilities poorer salespeople disliked, such as the constant need to keep up-to-date on a rapidly changing product line and a relatively long sales cycle. Some had to do with the job itself, others with the ways in which UnitedCo operates. I've got quite a list."

"So as a first step, we've organized the motivational facets of the job," Fred said. "Now we must learn how our candidates value those facets."

"How should we get information on it?" Paula asked.

Jimmy had an idea. "Once we've got our list of motivational facets, we can run down it and ask the candidates which they like and which they don't like."

"It might be more productive if we were a little less direct," Fred said. "We could ask for a time when a candidate was particularly satisfied with a job or situation—or particularly dissatisfied—and see if he mentions aspects that pertain or do not pertain to the job in question. If he's really excited only when certain situations exist and these situations don't exist in the job, he won't stick around. It's the mistake I made with Joe Jackson—there wasn't a fit between his likes and dislikes and the sales job."

"But the motivation has to jibe with Fred's specific job, right?" Jimmy answered his own question. "Say a guy got along lousy with people. You wouldn't hire him as a tour guide, but he'd be perfect as a lighthouse keeper."

Paula nodded in agreement. "People can't be classified as motivated or not motivated. Everyone is motivated by something. Motivation is relative to the specific job in question."

"Clearly, determining a candidate's motivations—and how they fit with the position—is highly important," Fred said. "Indeed, I suggest it stands as the second component of our system."

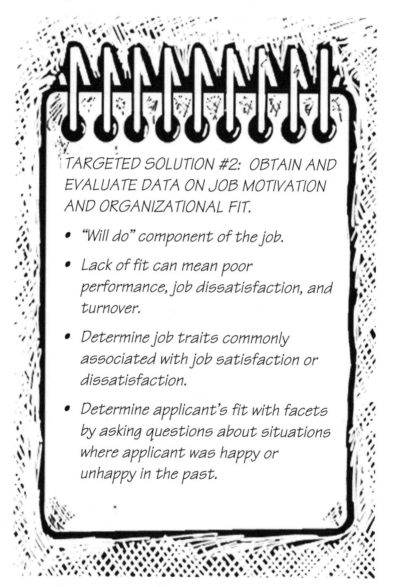

TARGETED SOLUTION #2: OBTAIN AND EVALUATE DATA ON JOB MOTIVATION AND ORGANIZATIONAL FIT.

- "Will do" component of the job.

- Lack of fit can mean poor performance, job dissatisfaction, and turnover.

- Determine job traits commonly associated with job satisfaction or dissatisfaction.

- Determine applicant's fit with facets by asking questions about situations where applicant was happy or unhappy in the past.

CHAPTER TEN

Fred checked his voice mail and found a message from Mort Saroyan, one of his four candidates. Mort asked if he could stop by to pick up some literature on UnitedCo's products.

"Tell him sure," Jimmy suggested. "Now that we've figured out our dimensions, it'll give us a chance to grill him." Jimmy caught Paula giving him a look. "Ask him a few polite questions, is what I meant," Jimmy amended.

Fred returned Mort's call and caught him as he was leaving his office, which was not far from UnitedCo. They agreed that Mort would stop by in a few minutes.

►

While awaiting Mort's arrival, Fred, Paula, and Jimmy reviewed Mort's application file.

"Mort has been in sales all his adult life, beginning by selling self-help books part-time while in college," Fred began. "Soon after graduation, he turned to insurance, made the President's Club eight out of the next ten years, and was among the top five salespeople in the nation for the last two. He's currently working for City Brokerage, specializing in financial planning, and he's earned the highest commissions in his region for the past six quarters."

Jimmy snorted skeptically. "Or so he says. Let's see how he stands up when we interview him."

Mort soon arrived. After Fred introduced Paula and Jimmy, Mort asked some questions about UnitedCo. Fred explained that the typical sale ranged from $20,000 to $50,000. The sales cycle was fairly long, especially with new customers or new products, and involved explanation of the products' advantages, often followed by several demonstrations to members of the client's technical staff and executives. The latter, rather than purchasing agents, were typically the decision makers.

"I've got some questions for you," Jimmy said when Fred was finished. "Why are you so attracted to sales?"

Mort smiled pleasantly. "You might say heredity. My grandfather sold oil leases in Montana and was darned good at it. My father began by selling brushes door to door—and ended up owning the brush company."

"So like the old saying goes, 'The apple doesn't fall far from the tree,'" interjected Jimmy.

"That's right," Mort agreed, "but besides being brought up by salesmen, I learned there was a lot of satisfaction in the job. Granddad was in a business considered to be somewhat shady, but he was honest, and most of his clients profited. Dad succeeded because his brushes were the best on the market. Like them, I love to sell—and also like them, I see sales as a contract dictating that both the buyer and seller benefit."

"Can you give me an example of how that has worked?" Fred inquired.

"When I was in insurance, I sold a disability policy to a young contractor who was a single father. Not six months later, he was badly injured in a fall from the roof of a garage he was building. Without that coverage he would have lost his home, and his children would have gone hungry. I felt darned good at my role in keeping that from happening."

"Did you ever face a tough sell?" Jimmy asked.

"All the time." Mort smiled in recollection. "One instance sticks in my mind from the early days when I sold self-help books. At first I didn't do well—but then I read the books myself. They really did give solid advice about taking charge of your own life, and I did. My sales increased."

"So you're the resilient type." Jimmy said,

remembering their list of dimensions. "Tell me how you talked someone into making a purchase."

"During that period I also sold encyclopedias," Mort said. "Nearly all my prospects were young couples with children and with limited budgets. So I had two tasks: first, to show them that my product would help the kids in school, and second, to devise a way they could afford it. So I convinced my regional manager to offer a longer-term payment plan."

"Did that work well?"

"I'll say," Mort nodded. "Part of my commission was deferred, but I more than offset that through increased sales. Not only that, but by offering the new payment plan I'd designed, the other salespeople also did better, and so did the company. I'd call that a win-win situation for all involved."

Fred said, "Could you describe a specific sale when that approach failed?"

Mort thought about it. "I can tell you when I had to go the extra mile," he said. "One couple had already sat through a sales pitch from my competitor, whose books were significantly less expensive. So even with my customized payment plan, it was going to be a difficult sale."

"What did you do?"

"Luckily, my competitor had left a sample volume for their perusal," Mort replied. "I compared it to ours, clearly demonstrating that, for somewhat more money, they'd get twice the depth of information, annual update volumes, and so forth." Mort smiled. "I made the sale, which pleased me a great deal. Later, I got a letter from the customer, reporting that he had gone back to school to finish his college education and was doing well. That made me feel great. The experience prompted me to buy my own set of the competitor's product so I could add the comparison to my standard sales pitch."

"Good for you." Jimmy found himself warming up to Mort, but he had a job to do, so he said, "But still, there must have been times when you went away empty-handed."

"Many times," Mort confirmed. "That's the nature of the game. I remember an executive who requested a meeting regarding a term-life policy. But when I kept our appointment, he was clearly preoccupied with other matters. Rather than waste his time and mine, I got out of there as quickly as was polite. You must know when to cut your losses."

Jimmy tried a question relating to the dimension of Planning and Organizing. "What would you do if you had too many sales calls scheduled on the same day?"

"I'd never let that happen," Mort said.

"Even if you did," Jimmy said, "I guess you'd figure a way to keep all your clients from feeling you were neglecting any of them."

"You bet," Mort replied.

That didn't seem especially helpful information to Fred, so he took a shot at the same dimension. "Mort, could you provide a few examples of how you followed up after making a sale?"

Mort looked a bit perplexed. "In the self-help and encyclopedia business, I usually didn't," he answered. "As I said, updates were included in the original purchase and shipped automatically to the customer. With a few clients, I did follow up in an attempt to place additional products, but most had limited income, and I didn't want to try to 'drink at the well' too often. It didn't seem an efficient use of my time."

"And when you were in insurance?"

"I'd watch the newspapers and business journals," Mort said, "and if I learned that someone's financial status had significantly improved, I checked in to see if they needed further coverage."

"Do you maintain contact with clients in your present position with the brokerage house?" Fred asked.

"Absolutely," Mort said. "I go over every client's portfolio at least monthly. If I see that an investment is performing poorly, I review my list of promising alternatives, and then call the client with my recommendation. Of course," Mort added quickly, "you've got to choose the times when you do that. I wouldn't want to give the impression I was 'churning' an account."

Paula smoothly cut in. "We've taken enough of your time for now, Mort." She thanked him, explained that she and Jimmy would be continuing to help Fred make his hiring decision, and said she looked forward to talking again as the hiring process progressed.

Once Mort left, Jimmy could not conceal his pleasure. "This behavior stuff isn't so tough. Look at all we learned with a few questions."

Paula rose. "We'll discuss that in due time, Kid," she said.

CHAPTER ELEVEN

Back at Paula's office, Jimmy said into the phone, "How'd Galloping Gertie do in the third race, Maloney?" He listened and grunted, "Thanks for nothing," then slammed down the receiver.

"What's wrong?" Fred asked.

"I lost a two-spot," Jimmy complained. "Galloping Gertie finished dead last."

"I'm surprised she did that badly," Paula said, "after what Mack told you."

"It's what he didn't tell me," Jimmy complained. "Now I find out from Maloney that all of her wins were in six-furlong sprints on dry tracks. Yesterday's race was a mile and a quarter, and before post time a cloudburst turned the racecourse into gumbo." He shook his head. "That darned swaybacked fermented buskirk of a nag!"

Fred whistled. "That boy's got some mouth on him."

Paula called in an order for some snacks from Hors D'oeuvres to Go as Jimmy readdressed himself to the case. "Something's puzzling me," he said. "Why are we focusing on the past? We should be asking questions about what each of our suspects will do in the new job—if they get it."

Paula matched his question with another. "Why did you bet on Galloping Gertie?"

"Because she won before," Jimmy said. "I suppose if you want to put it in the terms we've been tossing around, she had the dimension of speed, which I'd say is relevant to horse race success. But that didn't mean a win this time, because I didn't learn the whole story before betting."

Paula turned to Fred. "Why did you hire me?"

"The newspaper said you were the best detective in town," Fred said. "And you did solve The Case of The Chameleon, involving an impostor much like the one I'm facing."

"So we're talking about a 'track record.' Pardon the pun," Jimmy added. "If a person—or horse—consistently does certain things, we figure she'll continue to do the same things."

"That's certainly true," Fred agreed. "In fact, people use past behavior to predict future behavior all the time."

"We do?"

"Certainly," Fred said. "When you approach a banker for a loan, she wants to see your past payment history," he said. "A scientist who applies for a grant is more likely to get it if he demonstrated prior progress in that field of research."

"Or if you're under suspicion," Jimmy chimed in, "the coppers check out your rap sheet."

Fred began to take notes. "It occurs to me, Paula, that in evaluating people for hiring, promotion, or a pay increase, we often consider statistics—an advertising executive's number of satisfied clients, a truck driver's traffic offenses, even a baseball player's batting average. And all these statistics reflect past behaviors."

"Don't forget, just as Jimmy mentioned, we also make judgments when past behaviors are negative," Paula pointed out. "You wouldn't go back to a barber who gave you an ugly haircut, or a saloon where the bartender was rude."

"Then why do we hang out at Maloney's?" Jimmy wisecracked. "Anyway, so what? Take Mort. He says he made a lot of sales and plenty of money for himself and his company, and he won a lot of awards. So he's a great salesman and you should hire him, Fred—or he's a bald-faced liar and we should arrest him, Paula. But I'll be a sprung-gutted polecat if anything we've learned tells us which he is."

"Let's talk about what we have learned," Paula suggested.

"For starters," Jimmy said, "Mort loves to sell."

"You'd hardly expect a person applying for a sales job to say he doesn't like to sell," Fred noted dryly.

"That's my point, Fred," Jimmy said. "Mort gave us reasons for liking sales. I think the pleasure he claims to get in helping clients is genuine, like that story about the contractor's kids who didn't go hungry."

"I was impressed by that as well," Fred agreed, "and I have a notion about its significance. Remember how Mort began by telling us about his father and grandfather. Each was a scrupulous and successful salesperson with a high regard for his customers' welfare. I suggest that Mort has also been successful through an emotional need to emulate, and even exceed, the accomplishments of his father."

Paula held up a hand. "Let's slow down, fellas. I don't think either of you is really talking about behavior. Mort's enjoyment of sales and his pleasure at helping a client gets at motivation, but we really didn't intend to go after that dimension today. As to your theory of the influence of Mort's father, I sometimes took a similar approach when I started out as a detective, such as trying to analyze whether a suspect was the 'criminal type.' It didn't work.

I learned that it's difficult to 'play psychologist' without a lot of training, and if I did, I was more likely to jump to the wrong conclusions than to elicit information I could use."

Jimmy looked dejected. "I thought we got all sorts of useful information, and now it looks like we didn't learn a darned thing."

"I wouldn't say that," Paula encouraged.

CHAPTER TWELVE

They were interrupted by the arrival of Dukes Finnegan, proprietor of Hors D'oeuvres to Go, bearing a bag containing tofu dip; no-salt, fat-free corn chips; vegetarian egg rolls; and a bucket of Japanese chicken salad. Paula introduced Dukes to Fred while Jimmy tentatively tried the dip. "Just once I wish you'd patronize a joint with real food and drink," he grumbled at Paula, although to himself he admitted that the snacks were pretty tasty.

"Hey, Dukes," Jimmy said suddenly. "The other day Mack the Hack mentioned that you fought The Champ."

"That's right," Dukes affirmed. "I hit him with a roundhouse right, and he went down like a ton of wet cement."

"Too bad you're not still in the fighting game," Jimmy said. "I'd put a two-spot on you. You could have been a contender."

As Dukes started to leave, Fred said, "Excuse me, Dukes, but did you win that match?"

Dukes shook his head and grinned, revealing a gap where one of his front teeth had been. "In fact, that was my last fight," he said. "You see, at the time we were both 14 and competing in the Junior Gloves program, so The Champ wasn't 'The Champ' yet. After I knocked him down, he got back up and KO'd me 30 seconds later."

As Dukes went out, Jimmy checked his wallet. "I hope I get a handle on this system of yours soon, Paula," he said. "I'm running out of two-spots." Jimmy suddenly shot Fred a sharp look. "How did you know to ask Dukes how the fight turned out? Did you have some inside information and want to make me look like a chump?"

"Not at all, Jimmy," Fred said quickly. "Rather, I was thinking about the examples you got from Mort."

"What about them?" Jimmy demanded.

"Some of the information seemed incomplete. Pardon me, Jimmy, but take the story where Mort's sales of self-help books were poor until he read them, and then got better."

"That shows that he developed his Sales Ability," Jimmy said.

"Possibly, but in what context and to what degree? We know what he had to do—sell books. But we didn't really learn how he made sales, nor do we know how much better he did. It could have been that he succeeded with 1 out of 50 prospects before he changed his approach, and 2 out of 50 afterward. That would be a dim definition of success."

"It's also an exaggerated example," Jimmy protested.

"Granted, but it could be actual, for all we know," Fred said reasonably. "It's a situation where we failed to get complete information—and mind you, Jimmy, I'm not criticizing you. I could have asked more questions myself."

"Thanks, Fred," Jimmy said. "I guess we've both got a lot to learn."

"Mort told us about the time he stopped his sales pitch to the busy executive because he knew he wouldn't land the sale," Fred said. "But what happened after that? Did Mort follow up with a call or a letter saying he'd be happy to meet with the client again, at his convenience? Most salespeople would. Maybe Mort did, and it resulted in a sale—or it didn't. Or maybe he didn't follow up. Without knowing all the facts, we have little on which to base an evaluation of Mort's Sales Ability."

"But we know he's a good salesperson," protested

Jimmy. "He's won all those awards each year."

"I would guess those are legitimate," Fred responded. "But even there we could have gotten more information. What if there had been only one other salesperson in his region, or Mort had one big customer that produced the numbers he needed to win?"

"What about when I asked what he'd do if he scheduled too many calls?" Jimmy argued. "He said he'd never let that happen. Isn't that what a good salesperson does?"

"Kid, that's like asking a suspect, 'If you went to a dinner party where the cutlery wasn't nailed down, would you pocket some silverware?'" Paula said. "It's a theoretical question. *Would have* and *could have* are different from *did do, will do*, and *can do*."

"I can see how that would get you the answer that the person thought you wanted," Jimmy said. "It was the same when I followed up by saying that I was sure he'd never let his clients become dissatisfied. How was he supposed to answer?" Jimmy went on ironically. "That he would like dissatisfied clients?"

"Let me review here," Fred said, making further notes. "We agree that past behavior predicts future behavior, and that neither theoretical nor leading questions elicit valid information about behavior. Yet some of the questions we asked that did address behavior still didn't obtain the whole story."

"You've got to know what's going on, for starters,"

Jimmy said. "With Dukes' story about fighting The Champ, I assumed it was for the title, but in fact they were just kids."

"Then you must be clear on what ensued," Fred amplified. "You did all right on that—Dukes knocked down The Champ."

"But then you asked the question that got to the nitty-gritty," Jimmy picked up. "The knockdown didn't end the fight—it just got The Champ riled up enough to put Dukes down for the count."

Fred looked up. "In other words," he said, "for behavioral information to be complete, it must include three elements. First, we must know the Situation or Task, such as Dukes and The Champ facing each other in a teenage boxing match. Second is the Action—Dukes hit The Champ, and then The Champ KO'd Dukes. Third is the Result, which was that The Champ won and Dukes retired from the ring."

Fred finished writing. "A STAR is born," he declared.

"I get it, Fred," Jimmy said. "Your STAR idea will help us remember to get the whole story while interviewing. That way we'll know exactly how a person acted, and whether those actions were effective or unsuccessful, or even inappropriate to the situation."

"Exactly," Fred agreed. "And by knowing how a candidate behaved in the past, we'll have valuable data on how he will likely behave if hired for my position."

Fred showed Paula and Jimmy the most recent page of his notebook:

TARGETED SOLUTION #3: USE PAST BEHAVIOR TO PREDICT FUTURE BEHAVIOR.

- *By seeking complete STARs, theoretical questions are avoided.*

- *Behavioral STARs are the key to understanding past behavior, and they provide information that is much less likely to be misinterpreted.*

CHAPTER THIRTEEN

Jimmy scraped the last of the tofu dip from the container. "Here's something we haven't discussed." Jimmy turned to face Paula and Fred. "How do you like Mort for The Faker? He admitted he's lost a lot of sales."

"But that's par for the course," Fred pointed out.

"Exactly." Jimmy stalked across the room. "And any reasonably skilled faker would know that. Of course he'd say he'd lost sales."

"And that he'd made sales, as well," Fred said, "which he has—or says he has."

◄

Jimmy smacked his forehead, incidentally knocking his slouch hat sideways. "We're going in circles," he complained. "Like I said, Mort is lying or he isn't. How do we find out?"

Paula thought for a moment. "Well, let's assume that he is strong in sales," she said. "What does that tell us?"

"That he's not a faker and that he can sell!" In his frustration, Jimmy was close to apoplexy.

"But can he sell for me?" Fred asked himself quietly.

Jimmy gaped at him.

"Remember, Jimmy, Sales Ability is specific to sales situations. Door-to-door sales, where you have only one shot at a customer, is very different from relationship selling like we do. Our salespeople try to partner with our clients." Fred continued.

Jimmy nodded with comprehension. "That's how you solve mysteries, isn't it, Paula? You can't just ask the suspect if he did it. And even if he's committed crimes in the past, it doesn't mean he's guilty of this one. You have to get down to job-specific behavior, motivation, and knowledge."

"Yes," Paula replied. "And when I have that information for each of the target dimensions, there's bound to be data that adds up—or doesn't."

CHAPTER FOURTEEN

Because Fred had a social obligation that evening and Jimmy was going to the City Sluggers baseball game with Mack the Hack, the three of them adjourned. Fred's first formal interview, with the second candidate—Jennifer Lee—was scheduled for 11 o'clock the next morning. Paula, Fred, and Jimmy agreed to meet at 10 a.m. in Fred's office to further discuss strategies for getting all the information they'd need for each of the four candidates.

When 10:30 passed and Jimmy was nowhere to be seen, Paula suggested they go over Jennifer's file.

"I met her when, like Mort, she came in to ask some questions about the position," Fred began. "Unlike Mort, she was rather less diffident."

"In an off-putting way?" Paula asked.

"Not at all," Fred explained. "She basically said, 'Tell me what you are looking for, and if I'm not confident I can fit the bill, I won't waste your time.' She didn't put it as bluntly, of course, but the point is she was determining the 'client's' needs."

Paula reviewed her copy of Jennifer's file. "Her degree is in library science, but after one job in that field, all of her experience has been in sales. Each of her successive positions seems to be a step up."

"I'd say so," Fred agreed. "I'm familiar with the software firm where she is presently employed. Their customized products are highly sophisticated and priced at the high end, and they're marketed to equally sophisticated organizations. Hers is a challenging job, and she appears to have met the challenge."

"And your other impressions?"

"Primarily positive," Fred replied. "She's young and clearly physically fit, and she mentioned that she participates in several competitive sports. I found her ambitious and assertive—perhaps too assertive."

Jimmy came bustling in at 2 minutes to 11. "Mack had a flat tire," he explained.

"Jennifer will be here at any moment," Fred admonished.

"I also overslept," Jimmy admitted sheepishly. "The game went 15 innings. Then Bats Brannigan took a called strike on a three-and-two count, and Homeville beat us by a score of 5–4. I lost a two-spot to Mack, and I drowned my sorrows at Maloney's." Jimmy released a discreet belch. "I guess I hit the ginger ale pretty hard."

Susan, the secretary, announced that Jennifer had arrived and ushered her in. Jennifer used a wheelchair. After explaining the role of Paula and Jimmy in the interview, Fred began to ask questions designed to elicit behavioral examples in their dimensions. But Jimmy's ginger ale hangover distracted his attention. He'd never had the chance to speak with a disabled person and was filled with curiosity.

When Fred paused between inquiries, Jimmy jumped in with what he thought were polite, innocuous questions. He learned that Jennifer was 32 years old, married, and a lifelong resident of The City. But Jimmy sensed that, for some odd reason, Jennifer was a bit irritated at his queries, so he complimented her on how well she seemed to get around despite her chair.

"If you are asking whether my disability would affect my ability to fulfill the responsibilities of this position," Jennifer said, "the answer is no. I drive a specially equipped vehicle, and I'm sure the buildings of UnitedCo's clients are all accessible."

Fred, sensing big trouble, leaped to his feet, but he was too late. Jimmy was already asking, "So, why do you use a wheelchair?"

Jennifer gazed at him. "For the same purpose other people use their legs," she said.

Fred managed to wrest back control of the interview and asked a few more questions before he told Jennifer he would be calling her to schedule another session. Meanwhile, Jimmy had the sense to clam up, because he knew he was in trouble.

"Why's everyone looking at me?" he protested after Jennifer left. Jimmy had never seen Fred so upset. "What did I do?"

"While representing UnitedCo, you could have exposed our organization to an expensive lawsuit."

Fred paced the room until he felt more calm. "I apologize for blowing up at you, Jimmy. That wasn't very effective feedback on your inappropriate questions."

"What questions?"

"About age, marital status, length of residence, and finally, disability. Inquiry into such non-job-related subjects is a violation of Federal law."

"But the answers could provide clues."

"How so, Kid?" Paula asked. "Which of our dimensions do they concern?"

"None," Fred answered for Jimmy. "Aside from their

unfairness, your questions had absolutely nothing to do with dimensions important to the job."

"Oh yeah?" Jimmy argued. "What if she can't get around well enough?"

"You don't try to guess for her," Fred responded. "You describe the essential functions of the position and ask if, for any reason, she wouldn't be effective in them with reasonable accommodations. If she foresees a problem, you see if there's an accommodation that can be worked out. Her disability clearly hasn't been a difficulty during her successful 10-year career in sales," Fred continued, still a bit nettled, "as you would have known if you hadn't overslept."

Jimmy could see that Fred was right, and he apologized. When Fred offered coffee, Jimmy accepted with gratitude. "Maybe some hot java will irrigate my brain," he added morosely.

CHAPTER FIFTEEN

With Jimmy slumped contritely in his chair, Paula said to Fred, "Tell me how you go about hiring."

"We advertise in appropriate publications and register the job with government employment agencies," Fred said. "Human Resources screens the resumes we receive and conducts preliminary interviews to eliminate candidates who don't meet stated job requirements. For example, if we were hiring a delivery person, we'd require a valid driver's license. That's called 'knock-out data,' and it's the first 'decision point.'"

"Then you interview them?" Jimmy asked.

▶

"If I feel strongly positive or negative about a candidate, I do the only interview. In cases where my initial reaction is less clear-cut, I'll usually ask another manager or two to interview as well."

Fred stopped himself. "I criticized you for unfairness, Jimmy, but I guess what I just described isn't very fair either," he realized. "I've treated candidates unequally, based on my first impression."

Fred turned to Paula. "Do you have any suggestions?"

"You've pointed to the first one," Paula said. "What if each of us interviews all four of the candidates?"

"That sounds like an equitable approach," Fred said. "Giving some candidates the benefit of several interviews and others only one isn't fair. But won't that be time-consuming?"

"Let's divide up the dimensions that each of us will cover," Jimmy suggested. "How about if we each take four or five of the first seven—that'll provide us with backup and perspective. All three of us can cover Oral Communication and Impact, since we'll be observing behaviors in those dimensions, rather than asking questions about them."

Fred rose and went to a flip chart in the corner of his office. When Fred finished, the assignment chart looked like this:

	Fred	Paula	Jimmy
Persuasiveness/Sales Ability	X	X	
Resilience	X		X
Analysis		X	X
Planning and Organizing		X	X
Judgment	X		X
Initiative	X	X	
Motivational Fit	X	X	
Oral Communication	X	X	X
Impact	X	X	X

"You've worked it so each of us will ask questions about most of the first seven dimensions," Jimmy observed, "and each dimension is covered by at least two of us. That should work out fine."

Thinking about the assignment, Fred suggested, "While normally this sort of interview would be conducted one-on-one, perhaps during some of them, another of our little group can be present. That way we can give feedback to each other on our interviewing skills."

"That sounds like a helpful idea," Paula agreed.

Jimmy suddenly frowned. "But what questions do we ask? I'm thinking how with Joe Jackson I wanted to know about the same stuff Fred already covered, and then with Jennifer I got into illegal and unfair territory. And while we're on it, with Mort sometimes I forgot to get the whole story."

"Let's draft the questions we'll each ask." Fred got out his notebook and flipped back to the entry he'd made the previous day when they determined the relevant dimensions and their key actions. He copied the definition of Initiative and its key actions to the top of a fresh sheet. "This will help remind us what types of examples we're seeking from the candidates."

A lively discussion followed on what questions would best elicit complete, nontheoretical, behavioral information on the dimension. It took time, but they finally agreed on six queries, three for each of the interviewers assigned to seek examples in Initiative.

"This will ensure that our questions are challenging and don't overlap," Paula said, "and it allows us to concentrate on the candidates' answers, instead of worrying about what to ask next. Good idea, Fred."

"I've got another." Fred asked Susan to come in, sat her at his computer, and explained her assignment. "Susan is quite an artist when it comes to desktop publishing," he told Paula and Jimmy.

While Susan went to work, they turned to their other dimensions. Applying a good deal of mental "elbow grease," they came up with questions for each. "By the way," Fred said at one point, "let's bear in mind that these questions can be modified as the interview dictates. In fact, it seems to me that in some cases not every question must be asked. The important thing is to get several complete STARs in each dimension."

Jimmy thought about that. "I see what you mean. You could repeat a question to get another example of behavior rather than move on to another question. Or you might want to follow up on a lead you picked up on earlier in the interview."

Nodding his head, Fred said, "That's it."

As they finished up, Susan presented to Fred—with pardonable pride—her implementation of his idea.

Initiative—Making active attempts to influence events to achieve goals; self-starting rather than accepting passively; taking action to achieve goals beyond what is required; being proactive.

Key Actions
- Be proactive.
- Generate ideas for improvement.
- Solve problems without being asked.
- Take advantage of opportunities without being asked.
- Seek opportunities for self-improvement.
- Do more than required.

Planned Behavioral Questions

1. Have you suggested a new idea to someone recently? (What was the idea? What prompted the idea?)

2. What has been your biggest achievement at _____ ?

   (What steps did you take to achieve it?)

3. How did you get your job at _____ ?

Situation/Task	Action	Result

Communication _____

Impact _____

Initiative Rating: [ ]

"Great job, Susan!" Fred complimented. "Could you work up similar pages for each of our dimensions? Thanks."

Fred showed the page to Paula and Jimmy. "This puts some real organization and precision into our interviewing," Paula said. "It's bound to pay off."

"Speaking of payoffs . . ." Jimmy said. With Fred's permission he dialed a number from memory on Fred's phone.

Something occurred to Fred. "How do we keep track of the answers we get?" he asked Paula.

"What has worked for me is to take notes," she said.

Fred seemed skeptical. "Won't a candidate find that off-putting?"

"That's rarely the case in my experience, if I explain the purpose of notes," Paula said. "The notes provide an account of what the person *said*, not what I later *thought* he or she said. My note taking indicates that I consider the person's information to be important, meaningful, and deserving of an accurate record."

"That's true, and I'm sure if I explain it that way, it will help put the candidate at ease," Fred said.

Meanwhile, on the phone Jimmy said, "Maloney? Is Wickets Wiskowski still the favorite in the City Croquet Championships?" Jimmy listened to Maloney's inside information. Satisfied, he said, "Put a two-spot on him for me."

Jimmy hung up. "This Wiskowski character has taken

the crown three years running," he informed Paula and Fred, "and the tourney is at City Fields, his favorite croquet layout. He's a cinch to win." Jimmy grinned. "Paula, this system of yours is money in the bank."

"Let's not go overboard, Jimmy," the always-cautious Fred remarked. "But I will agree that we've now come up with the fourth crucial component of our system. I jotted it down while you were on the phone."

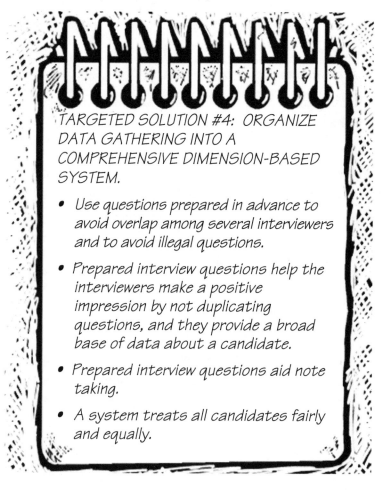

TARGETED SOLUTION #4: ORGANIZE DATA GATHERING INTO A COMPREHENSIVE DIMENSION-BASED SYSTEM.

- *Use questions prepared in advance to avoid overlap among several interviewers and to avoid illegal questions.*

- *Prepared interview questions help the interviewers make a positive impression by not duplicating questions, and they provide a broad base of data about a candidate.*

- *Prepared interview questions aid note taking.*

- *A system treats all candidates fairly and equally.*

CHAPTER SIXTEEN

Two candidates remained—Thomas Goldman and Millicent Matthews.

"I've scheduled an interview with Thomas for two o'clock this afternoon," Fred said to Paula. "Would you mind being present?"

"That's jake with me, Paula," Jimmy said. "I was thinking of arranging a get-together with this Millicent on my own."

"All right, Kid," Paula agreed. "But try to remember everything we've been discussing."

"Don't worry, Paula." Jimmy tried to sound casual, but he was eager to get the "first shot" at Millicent. He'd gone over her file closely, and what he saw made him increasingly excited.

Millicent was an excellent candidate—for The Faker! If Jimmy's legwork led to her unmasking, it would be a real feather in his slouch hat.

Millicent had no experience in sales whatsoever. In fact, she'd worked for only a short time after college as a teacher and school counselor, and after that she hadn't held any job at all for nearly 15 years. During that time she became involved with several charitable and civic organizations, and she served on both the school board and the town council of her 35,000-person suburb. But Jimmy couldn't see what all that had to do with sales.

He sure as heck could see what it had to do with fakery, though.

Jimmy deduced that The Faker might have feared that UnitedCo would check the accuracy of the job information he or she cited. And Millicent's stating that she hadn't worked for so long was convenient because it would be hard to contradict through legwork.

While Jimmy phoned Millicent to arrange a meeting, Fred and Paula reviewed Thomas Goldman's file. "He's the only one of the candidates I haven't met in person," Fred began, "but on paper he's nearly perfect for the position."

"I was also impressed," Paula said. "Like Mort, he's been in sales since graduating from college."

"In a manner of speaking, he was 'in sales' even in college," Fred said. "His major was business, and he was president of his fraternity and president of the student senate, so he must have been persuasive and well liked."

Jimmy rejoined them and reported that he'd reached Millicent. "She's on her way to a luncheon meeting of the Waterfront District Renewal Project," he said. "She asked if we could get together at Maloney's after that."

Returning to Thomas' resume, Fred noted other similarities to Mort, including making his organization's Sales Round Table nearly every year and winning many awards and bonuses. "Where Thomas' career diverges from Mort's is in the products he sold, which are significantly more similar to those of UnitedCo."

"It says here he began as a marketing trainee at Fenwick Package Goods," Jimmy noted. "Do they do a good job of developing people?"

"I'm told they do," Fred said. "And while at Fenwick, Thomas supplemented their program with outside courses in sales effectiveness. He was with Fenwick for a half-dozen years before leaving for his present job with Universal, our main competitor."

"Aha!" Jimmy gave them a significant look. "So why is he leaving?"

"We'll have to ask him that," Paula said. "But according to Mack the Hack, Universal has instituted some reorganization measures lately."

"Mack sure has his finger on the pulsebeat of the corporate world," Jimmy said with a touch of sarcasm. "Has it occurred to anyone besides me that this resume might be a little too perfect?"

"Actually, Jimmy," Fred said, "that applies in some degree to the resumes of three of our candidates. Mort, Jennifer, and Thomas all have outstanding sales records, while Millicent . . ."

"And for that reason, they are all suspicious," Jimmy interrupted. He didn't want Fred or Paula to hit on his theory about Millicent until he had a chance to check it out. "The point is that any one of them might be a liar. At least now we've got a system for pinning him or her down."

"And so?" Paula prompted.

"We need more dope on dimensions." Jimmy stood. "And I'm on my way to get some."

"Are you sure you won't join us for lunch?" Fred asked.

"No thanks," Jimmy said. "After that mystery meat I had yesterday, I'm sticking to food I can identify."

As he started out, Paula said, "Good luck with Millicent, Kid."

Jimmy gave her a big grin. "I'd say with our system, Paula, we're taking luck right out of the equation."

And Paula had to admit he was right.

CHAPTER SEVENTEEN

Fred's first impression of Thomas Goldman confirmed the positive feeling that his resume had imparted. Thomas was a tall, attractive man dressed neatly but not ostentatiously, with a fresh haircut and a firm handshake.

Fred started the interview with a brief review of Thomas' background, during which he asked the question Jimmy had brought up before lunch. "Would you mind telling me why you left your position at Fenwick?"

"The company twice reduced the size of my territory," Thomas replied. "I wasn't very pleased with that—what salesman would be?

A similar situation has come up in my present position, and it seems a good time to consider something new. It's too bad for both me and the organization," Thomas added. "I was tops in my division for five years, and believe me, I loved winning those trips to the Caribbean!"

"I notice that during your time at Universal," Fred said, "you worked as a district sales manager for a year."

"And I got restless as heck," Thomas said frankly. "I needed the adrenaline rush of being on the front lines."

"So you prefer working on your own as a salesperson?"

"Actually, in my experience I'm happier with team selling," Thomas amended. "I like collaborating with my colleagues, not only on the sales team but with people in technical support, research and development, and marketing. When a team pulls together and succeeds, it's satisfying to every member."

Fred was pleased to hear that, because UnitedCo was in the process of moving in that sales direction. Continuing with Motivational Fit, he learned that Thomas seemed happy in dealing with paperwork and other necessary but nonselling activities such as meetings and "skull sessions." Thomas also was clearly ambitious. He told them how he'd once worked 60-hour weeks for three months to earn enough commissions to make a down payment on a vacation home his wife had her heart set on. "She deserved it, after putting up with me," Thomas joked.

Fred turned to Sales Ability. "Tell me about an instance where you took an innovative approach to making a sale."

"I can give you two," Thomas said promptly. "In the first my company had been trying to crack an organization without success. The issue was price. Finally, I got an inquiry about a small order from a division of the organization. I took the risk of offering the large-volume discount applicable to the entire organization."

"What happened?" Fred followed up.

"The client bought, and soon the rest of the company signed on as well."

"That must have been gratifying," Fred said, as he made a note.

"So was the second case," Thomas said. "The person with buying authority was the purchasing manager, and while both he and I were certain my product would benefit his company, he was only authorized to sign a purchase order for up to $10,000—but this was a $70,000 product. So I got the idea of breaking the bill down into seven parts with successive monthly account due dates. We took a slight hit on the present value of the extended receivable, but we made up for it on repeat orders."

Before Fred could comment, Thomas said, "Here's one more I just thought of. A prospect questioned the price of a new state-of-the-art device, so I offered a full refund on a large order if it didn't turn out to be cost effective. Once again I was taking a chance, because if my tactic failed, we'd be significantly overstocked. But I felt I knew what I was doing, and it did the trick."

Noting that this STAR fell more into Judgment, Fred made a marginal note, then elicited a third STAR in Sales Ability. He continued with his other assigned dimensions, and Thomas helpfully provided data. Although Thomas reiterated his distaste for his brief stint as a manager, Fred was impressed that even there he'd performed well—on one occasion realigning sales territories, on another coming up with a training strategy for his staff, and on a third deftly handling a personnel conflict.

The STARs Fred obtained struck him as strongly positive, but then, seeking data in Resilience, Fred asked Thomas to describe a disappointment.

"A client seemed quite interested in our product," Thomas began, "and met with me a half-dozen times, often in the company of people from other divisions of his organization. They asked many technical and needs-related questions, and I spent a lot of time and hard work providing them with answers. But in the end they decided not to buy."

"That does sound like a disappointment," Fred sympathized.

"It was that, all right." Thomas smiled, but not with good humor. "Here's the rest of the story: Three months earlier, one of my colleagues had sold the same product to a different organization—and soon after, it filed for

Chapter 7. At the bankruptcy sale, my so-called client bought the nearly new product, at a fraction of what I would have had to charge. Throughout the sales cycle, he was exploiting me as an information source, with no intention of purchasing from me. Not only that, but he was also exploiting my colleague's mistake in extending credit to a soon-to-be-insolvent company. He got a huge bargain, and my organization got stuck with 10 cents on the dollar."

"How did you feel about that?"

"Angry and used," Thomas said a bit curtly.

"What did you do?"

Thomas shrugged. "What could I do? I put it out of my mind and waded back into the fray."

Fred asked two more questions and a follow-up to gain STARs in Resilience. He thanked Thomas and explained that Paula and Jimmy also would contact him by the next day to arrange interviews. Thomas shook hands all around and said he'd look forward to hearing from them.

"Did that story about the double-dealing client strike you as odd?" Fred asked Paula after Thomas left.

"In what way?"

"Thomas truly seemed impassioned," Fred said. "It was almost as if he took it personally. And yet at the end, he seemed suddenly to shrug it off."

"That's a good point to keep in mind when we look at his data as a whole," Paula said.

Fred nodded. "I wonder how Jimmy is doing?"

"So do I," Paula said wryly.

CHAPTER EIGHTEEN

J immy had been at Maloney's only long enough to down a stiff ginger ale when Millicent appeared at his corner table. "You were right, Mr. Swift," she said. "I had no trouble recognizing you. Isn't that trench coat kind of warm for this weather?"

Jimmy offered a drink. At the bar he ordered the carrot juice she requested, along with another ginger ale for himself. "What's a low-rent gumshoe like you doing with a classy tomato like Millicent?" Maloney sneered.

"Whaddaya know about her?" Jimmy demanded.

▶

"Born in Hightown, went to Lincoln High and State University," Maloney said. "In her spare time she does crossword puzzles, takes long walks, and not long ago she was in a production at City Playhouse."

"All right."

"Two kids, one . . ."

"I said all right." As Jimmy turned from the bar, something Maloney just mentioned sunk in. "Did you say she was an actress?"

"Yeah. What of it?"

Jimmy returned deep in thought on this new piece of information. But he decided to play his cards close to the vest for the time being. He began the interview by sticking close to his prepared questions, starting with the key issue of why, having never been in sales, Millicent thought she could be good at it.

"I'm not sure I will be," Millicent replied. "But when my second child began high school and I decided to re-enter the workforce, I analyzed the skills I'd developed in my nonprofit work. I realized that, in fact, I was involved in 'selling' my ideas."

That seemed a stretch to Jimmy, so he asked her for an example.

"For two terms I was on the city council of the suburb we live in. Once, we placed a four-mill levy on the ballot so we could buy the last piece of undeveloped land in the city and build a park," Millicent said. "It was a great chance to improve our recreation facilities for our children, and as a former teacher, I knew the importance of getting students off the streets. The Senior Citizens Organization, which represented enough votes to defeat the levy, was solidly against it because it meant increased real estate taxes."

"I read about it in the *News-Gazette*," Jimmy recalled. "Most of the seniors live on fixed incomes."

"Exactly," Millicent said. "So I had to convince them that they would receive a tangible financial benefit."

"How did you do that?"

"I researched small municipalities similar to ours, which had passed such levies," Millicent explained. "That produced several compelling arguments. First, the data showed that a solid tax base leads to maintaining property values. Second, strong and well-regarded recreation facilities attract newcomers to a community, buoying the real estate market. Third, we could make the park highly appealing for older adults to use and still make it a fun place for children."

Millicent smiled with pride. "It worked. The seniors supported the ballot issue, it passed, and everyone realized the anticipated benefits."

In response to Jimmy's further probing, Millicent told him how she was instrumental in attracting the relocation of the order fulfillment division of a catalog sportswear firm. She'd also persuaded a holding company to convey title to an abandoned railroad right of way, and then organized a successful fund-raising subcommittee to obtain private donations for converting the railbed into a network of urban bike-and-hike paths.

"I can see how what you've done is a sort of selling," Jimmy said, "but as to the actual sales game . . ."

Jimmy drew up short and muttered, "Game!" and excused himself. At the bar he learned from Maloney that Wickets Wiskowski had placed second in the croquet tourney. As Wickets was within a stroke of the home peg, an opponent hit his ball with a lucky shot and sent it into the rough.

"I'll be a ring-tailed birkenstock!" Turning toward the table, he noticed that Millicent looked a bit impatient with him, so he quickly returned and apologized, explaining about the lost bet.

"My sympathies, Mr. Swift," she said.

"Call me Jimmy," he said as he quickly got back to business. "I started to ask how you came to decide that the experiences you've described make you right for this particular sales job at UnitedCo."

"I didn't," Millicent said, to Jimmy's surprise. "My application was for public relations work, but the people in your human resources department thought I might be suitable for Mr. Hunt's opening."

Falling into being a finalist candidate like that seemed to indicate pretty poor motivation, but because that wasn't one of Jimmy's assigned dimensions, he noted it and moved on. In the course of the interview, Millicent mentioned that she felt her verbal skills weren't as good as they could be because she didn't always succeed in persuading others to her viewpoint.

Having covered his dimensions and in the course of wrapping up the interview, Jimmy made a complimentary comment about how much "work" Millicent had done while supposedly not actually "working." In doing so, he inadvertently elicited another example of behavior, and by now he was astute enough to recognize a STAR when it dropped into his lap.

"I did have a lot of demands on my time," Millicent said in response to his remark. "My children were heavily involved in school, sports, and extracurricular activities. I also chose to support my husband while he established his law practice, by volunteering to take over most of the household and family responsibilities. I had to plan carefully and organize my time."

"I guess you were juggling a lot of balls," Jimmy said.

Millicent nodded. "Each Sunday I made a chart of everyone's activities for the week, and from it I determined when I could make free time for myself, when I must see to the kids' needs, when my husband could cover for me, and so on. That system seemed to work because on only one occasion—and it involved an unforeseeable emergency—did I miss a meeting I'd promised to attend."

Jimmy had to admit to himself that was a pretty strong STAR in Planning and Organizing. In fact, he got many positive and complete STARs as he continued the interview.

When he finished, Jimmy set aside his notes, smiled pleasantly, and said, "Maloney tells me you're an actress."

"I have acted, yes." Millicent immediately sounded guarded.

"The reason I ask," Jimmy said cagily, "is because it seems to me that acting and sales have things in common. In both cases you're 'on stage' and you have to sell yourself to your audience."

Millicent hesitated for several moments. "I'm afraid I must go," she said finally.

Jimmy stood, thanked Millicent for her time, and walked her to the door. In response to Jimmy's phone call, Mack the Hack picked him up a few minutes later. As he climbed in, Mack gave him the once-over and said, "You look like you've been embraced by the arms of a dilemma, Sherlock."

"Aw, pipe down, Mack," Jimmy said. "I've got serious detective business on my mind."

CHAPTER NINETEEN

J immy joined Paula and Fred at the counter of Eats, a recently opened diner. Jimmy was pleased to find himself in a typical "greasy spoon." "Finally, a place where a guy can get some normal food," he said. "I'll have a plate of ham and eggs."

Mabel, the waitress, pointed at the bill of fare on the chalkboard behind the counter. It was headed "Your Friendly Neighborhood Vegetarian Joint."

"Bring us a couple of bagels with reduced-fat cream cheese," Paula said. Fred ordered dry whole-wheat toast and a glass of skim milk.

Mabel went to the cut-out window that connected to the kitchen. "Two kosher donuts, slather 'em light," she hollered. "A brown raft, landlocked, and a beaker of moo juice, hold the whey."

Jimmy suddenly noticed that Fred looked morosely preoccupied. "Why the long face?" he inquired.

"I've had a distinctly disturbing experience," Fred said. "As I was leaving UnitedCo just now, I stopped by our Human Resources Department to review a file. It was after hours by then, and I expected the office to be empty, but one person was in fact present—Thomas Goldman."

"What was he doing?" Jimmy gulped.

"Sitting at Bob Franklin's desk. Bob's one of our Human Resources people." Fred paused dramatically. "He was using Bob's computer."

"Mother of Garfield!" Jimmy exclaimed. "What was his explanation?"

"That's what I wanted to know," Fred said, "and I questioned him rather sternly. In fact, he was playing Gobble-Gal."

Paula was following this conversation with interest.

"Say what?" Jimmy asked.

"Thomas said that, during his first interview, he and Bob found they had a mutual interest in magic tricks. And since he was in the building toward the end of the work day, Thomas had invited Bob to visit a new magic store that just opened."

"A likely story," Jimmy scoffed.

"Yet it appears to be true," Fred said. "Bob returned from photocopying some documents he needed to go over at home this evening. He confirmed that he and Thomas were going to the magic store and that he'd invited Thomas to occupy himself by playing the computer game while he was busy."

"Are you sure he was really playing Gobble-Gal?" Paula asked.

"Oh yes," Fred replied. "I saw the screen."

"Thomas' explanation seems a little too convenient to me," Paula noted. "We'll have to keep this occurrence in mind."

"It is somewhat bothersome," Fred added.

Paula turned to Jimmy. "How did your interview with Millicent go?"

In light of Fred's story about Thomas, Jimmy had almost forgotten the suspicious new data he had on Millicent. He quickly told Fred and Paula about her acting background.

"What do you make of it?" Paula asked.

"Several things," Jimmy said. "Number one, by definition, The Faker has to be good at acting."

"But the converse isn't necessarily true," Fred noted. "Because Millicent is good at acting doesn't make her The Faker."

"Sure," Jimmy said, "but she seemed upset that I'd learned about it, and she clearly didn't want to pursue the discussion. That to me is highly suspect. I'd argue that a good actress has to have something of a pardonable ego and would jump at the chance to discuss all the roles she starred in."

"How was the interview otherwise?" Paula asked.

"Not bad, but not great either," Jimmy admitted. "At one point I jumped up to check on a bet, and I could tell she didn't like that I wasn't giving her all my attention."

"That is an important insight," Fred interjected. "I used to allow phone calls and even other people from the company to interrupt my interviews—until I went through some interviews for an overseas assignment in our company, and people did that to me. I felt that the interviewers didn't care about me because they thought the interruptions were more important than my interview. I was so upset that I turned down the job when it was offered. I decided I didn't want to work with those people. But it turned into a learning experience because I've been very careful about how I treat candidates ever since."

"What do you mean?" Jimmy asked.

"Making sure candidates know what to expect during

their visit to our office, that the receptionist is expecting them, that all the interviewers have the interviewee's background information and their interview assignments, and that the candidate's day is well planned. For example, I try to arrange for the candidate to have lunch with one of our salespeople so that the candidate can ask questions that he or she is reluctant to ask me," explained Fred. "Of course, things are a little different in filling this sales job, but I've tried to do my best to ensure UnitedCo makes a good impression."

"Speaking of making a good impression," Jimmy interjected, "another area of my interview that caused me concern was the note taking. It seemed like if I spent all that time on writing stuff down, it made it appear that I wasn't concentrating on her."

"I felt the same constraint with Thomas," Fred said. "It appeared I was doing a lot of writing, and I soon found I was only noting his most positive examples, since I conceived him as a strong candidate to start with."

"Note taking is a skill, and I had to practice to get it down," Paula said. "And I agree with you, Jimmy, that the way you do it can send messages to the interviewee."

"Especially if you start scribbling when they say something negative," Jimmy said. "If I were the candidate, that would make me squirm."

"You could wait a bit before making the note," Fred suggested. "Pick a time when the note taking would have no meaning. For example, if a candidate has just talked to you about being fired, you could wait to make notes on it until he talks about a happier subject, such as his success in immediately getting another job."

"That's a good idea," Jimmy agreed. "Still, writing all this stuff takes a lot of time."

"It doesn't have to," Paula said. "All you need is sufficient notes to provide recall of the STAR later, when we evaluate our data. For instance, to cover the Situation, Action, and Result in the mill levy example from Millicent, you might write: 'seniors resistant—analysis of other data showed them advantages—seniors convinced, tax passed.'"

"That sounds like it would work," Jimmy said. "So tell me about your session with Thomas. Did he pan out in person as well as he looked on paper?"

"I feel he did," Fred said. "For starters he had a firm handshake. I like that in a person."

"I've met many charming people with firm handshakes," Paula said. "Several of them are now behind bars."

For a moment Paula's analogy eluded Fred, but then he saw her point. "I suppose a handshake doesn't have much to do with predicting job-related behavior." He rechecked his notes. "It's a good thing I got many other STARs relative to the dimensions."

As Fred consulted his notes, he continued, "But I see now that by skimming over the negatives I missed some STARs as well. As Thomas and Mort both correctly noted, even the greatest salesperson in creation isn't going to hit a home run every time he steps up to bat. I should have delved more thoroughly into lost sales."

"I'm wondering, Fred," Paula said, "if a story about a client that did not purchase must necessarily be negative."

"It doesn't have to be," Jimmy said. "What if, after learning the customer's needs, you decided your product was wrong for her—and said so. That would show good judgment, because a dissatisfied customer wouldn't buy from you again. But one that you saved from making a bad choice might keep you in mind for other products."

Fred nodded. "Or the failure was caused by an ineffective, inappropriate, or otherwise inadequate presentation. But possibly you reviewed the situation, correctly identified your errors, and by not repeating them, improved your record."

"We've got three things going here," Jimmy pointed out. "First, we can't make 'snap' decisions based on a firm handshake, or even on some strong STARs early in the interview. If we do, then we're less likely to look for complete info on everything—positive and negative."

Mabel returned with their orders and said, "Enjoy."

"Second," Jimmy went on, "a negative result—no sale— isn't bad or good by itself. It's the situation and the behaviors along with the result that tell the tale."

Jimmy tried his bagel. "Third, you might jump to the conclusion that no sale means a negative in Sales Ability.

But actually, it could have to do with all sorts of dimensions—Resilience, Planning and Organizing, even Motivational Fit. The circumstances of the story can point you in the direction of more information in other areas—and again, it could be positive or negative."

"That's great, Jimmy." Fred looked up from writing in his notebook. "The way you're nailing down the finer points of interviewing, maybe you should apply for a position in UnitedCo's Human Resources Department."

Fred was kidding, but Jimmy gave him a scowl anyway. "No dice," he said. "Detecting is in my blood."

"You might be right, Kid, given the way you've helped us come up with our system," Paula said supportively.

"And at that task," Fred added, "we're making real progress in pinning down our Targeted Solutions."

In the notebook entry, Fred had written:

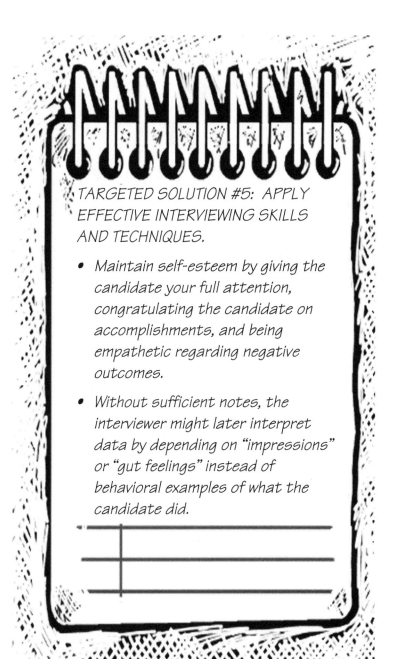

TARGETED SOLUTION #5: APPLY
EFFECTIVE INTERVIEWING SKILLS
AND TECHNIQUES.

• Maintain self-esteem by giving the
  candidate your full attention,
  congratulating the candidate on
  accomplishments, and being
  empathetic regarding negative
  outcomes.

• Without sufficient notes, the
  interviewer might later interpret
  data by depending on "impressions"
  or "gut feelings" instead of
  behavioral examples of what the
  candidate did.

CHAPTER TWENTY

I n the next few days, Paula, Jimmy, and
Fred continued their interviews, and as
their skills improved, some intriguing
clues to The Faker mystery began to emerge.
None was conclusive, and the three tried not
to jump to assumptions until all the
information was in; but still, patterns were
emerging.

"I'm concerned about two things," Jimmy
said on Friday morning as they met in Fred's
office. "First is the key dimension of Sales
Ability. Well, each of our four suspects 'talks a
good game.' Have you noticed any glaring
inconsistencies?"

"None that seem significant," Fred replied.

Jimmy continued, "While some of the four show stronger behaviors than others—and that's to be expected—none has told us a story that makes no sense in the context of sales."

"Except for Millicent's lack of experience," Paula noted.

"That gets to my second quandary," Jimmy said. "Motive." As was his habit, Jimmy was pacing the office by now. "Why would someone want to be a faker?"

"To gain employment," Fred said.

"I think it goes deeper than that," Jimmy insisted.

"What's your point, Kid?" Paula asked.

"I'm saying that the game is afoot."

"I thought Sherlock Holmes said that," Fred put in.

"Actually, Sir Arthur Conan Doyle adapted the line from Shakespeare's *Henry V*," Paula said.

Jimmy gaped at her. "How did you know that?"

"Detective work," Paula teased. "Go on, Kid."

"All of our suspects are intelligent and forceful to a significant degree," Jimmy elucidated. "None would have that much trouble landing a job he or she is really qualified for. So why does The Faker want this job he or she *isn't* qualified for?"

Jimmy answered his own question. "The Faker's motive is the game. The Faker wants to pull this off to show that he or she *can* pull it off. It's not about getting a job and then succeeding in the job—we all agree that won't happen. It's about bamboozling us."

Paula suddenly sat up straighter in her chair. "You've got something there, Kid. But why? Out of a sheer love of trickery?"

"Sure."

Paula took on a thoughtful look. "I say that trickery has a purpose."

Jimmy stared at her. "Do you know something you're not telling us?"

"It's only a hunch, but your theory put me on to it."

Jimmy was pleased and exasperated at the same time. He was sure Paula had come up with an important clue—and knowing her, she was going to play it close to the vest for the moment. Since trying to worm it out of her would do no good, he changed the subject to Jennifer.

The assertive attitude on which Fred had commented was borne out in Jimmy's interview with her. Her forthrightness was somehow unsettling. "At one point she told me that if she got the position, she'd do a fine job for UnitedCo," Jimmy reported. "If not, it wouldn't be the end of the world. The implication was almost that if she wasn't hired, it was our loss. I see two ways to interpret that. Maybe she is genuine and feels the need to compensate for her disability—or maybe she is challenging us to unmask her as The Faker."

"But again, that's playing psychologist," Fred said. "Where's the behavioral support?"

Jimmy paused in his pacing for dramatic effect, because he had a bombshell to drop.

"I'll tell you a behavior," he declared. "I saw her walk."

"My goodness!" Fred exclaimed.

"Under what circumstances?" Paula asked.

"After I interviewed her in Fred's office, I tailed her out to her van," Jimmy said. "She drove her chair into the back, then moved to the driver's seat."

Paula thought about that. "Different disabilities affect different people in different ways," she said. "If you'd spotted her running a marathon, I'd be a lot more suspicious, but walking a short distance, perhaps with the help of a support bar, hardly proves she's The Faker."

Jimmy felt frustrated once more, so he turned to Thomas Goldman. "Fred, I did manage to get one possible negative on Thomas. One time he missed a sales appointment when his secretary printed out the wrong day on his computerized calendar. That's a potentially costly mistake. And also, he covered it by pleading illness, which I'd consider risky judgment. On the other hand, he got away with it, and actually made the sale."

Jimmy turned on his heel. "My top suspect is still Millicent. She has no experience, she fell into applying for the position, and she doesn't have much confidence in her ability to do it. And look at her lousy communication skills."

"I thought she communicated quite well," Paula said.

"You missed the boat on this one," Jimmy said smugly. "Millicent told me to my face that she wasn't good."

"Did you have any trouble understanding her, Kid?" Paula said.

"I guess not," Jimmy said. "And she has made a lot of successful public presentations. But why would she say she communicated poorly?"

"That doesn't matter, Jimmy," Fred suggested. "It's like my point that all sales applicants say they'd do a good job of selling. But we're not interested in what they say. It's what they've done."

Fred consulted his notes. "As to her confidence, it seemed to build as the hiring process continued. When I spoke with her, she seemed much more comfortable with the idea that she actually could succeed in the position."

"Which could be just the kind of act The Faker would put on," Jimmy said. "You pretend to be self-effacing, and then you rise to the occasion."

"What about Mort?" Fred said. "From what you two have told me, I'm glad my formal interview with him is still to come, because something that arose the first time he came to the office has been bothering me."

"What's that?" Jimmy asked.

"When I asked him about following up with customers," Fred said, "he suggested that in book sales he thought it would be 'pushy.' That's an odd reaction for a salesperson. Your best sales opportunities are always people who have bought something from you already—and besides, it conflicts with Mort's satisfaction in helping clients."

Paula checked her watch. She had a dentist appointment at the same time as Mort's interview, but she assured Fred of her confidence that he'd do well in getting more information on the issues raised. At Fred's request, Jimmy agreed to sit in and provide feedback, while Paula invited them to join her when she met with Jennifer later that morning.

Jimmy especially looked forward to it. It finally appeared that they were on their way to a solution for this mystery.

CHAPTER TWENTY-ONE

P aula left for the dentist, and Mort arrived at Fred's office soon after. In beginning the interview, Fred requested, "Mort, tell me more about your likes and dislikes when it comes to sales."

"For one thing, sales is a numbers game," Mort replied, "and as you know, I've achieved excellent numbers. I'm pleased that I have succeeded, both for myself and my employer."

Fred realized that he'd asked a theoretical question and gotten a theoretical answer, so he tried to pin down a more useful response. "Can you tell me about a sale that provided particular satisfaction?"

◄

"When I went to work as a financial services consultant with City Brokerage," Mort began, "I analyzed the categories of financial instruments for performance, how each reacted to the economy, its risk, and so on. I also drew up a checklist that I used to analyze the client's needs. That way I could match one to the other."

Fred made a note as Mort continued. "That system was quite helpful with one particular client, an author who received $300,000 when one of his books was purchased by a movie producer. It was by far the biggest payday of his career, and while he might have been a good writer, he knew nothing about investment. You know, the sort who depends on hot tips from cab drivers."

Jimmy scowled, remembering his bet on Galloping Gertie.

"The writer had a list of stocks where he wanted to sink the entire amount," Mort said. "All were highly speculative. I advised him to invest the bulk of his windfall in conservative money market accounts and the remainder in a diversified growth fund. He was highly resistant.

"I sure as heck didn't want to lose a very large commission," Mort went on, "but I also didn't want him to lose his money. Referring to the information I had collected about the client, I mentioned that he had said that he often spent several years writing a book, during which time he had no income at all. I showed him what would happen if his stocks took a nose-dive, and alternatively, what would happen if he conserved his principal."

"Did he take your advice?" Fred asked.

"Yes," Mort said proudly, "though with reluctance. I didn't see him for a year, during which time the speculative stocks he had his eye on tumbled, while the mutuals I'd chosen appreciated and paid substantial dividends. Then one day, he came to the office to thank me. Instead of being dead broke, he was financially whole. Using his nest egg as collateral, he'd bought a nice bungalow, married his high school sweetheart, and was soon to be a proud father with the security of knowing he could provide for his family despite his rather dicey profession."

"That's great, Mort," Fred said. "And thanks—that's the kind of information I'm looking for." Jimmy noted how Fred's comments helped maintain Mort's self-esteem and how it encouraged him to give full behavioral examples. "Did you continue to manage this author's account?"

Mort smiled. "To be honest, just by the skin of my teeth," he said. "I had a lot on my mind the day he came in, and I neglected to ask how his writing was going. The very next day, I opened the *News-Gazette* to the books section and found a big feature article about how he'd received a half-million dollar advance on his next novel, which was predicted to be a best-seller. I got him on the horn right away, and I wasn't surprised that after the publicity, he'd been solicited by all sorts of brokers seeking his account."

"So you were up against some tough competition," Fred said.

Mort nodded. "I sat down with him, and we went over the proposals he'd received. That was a tough sell, because several were quite well thought out. And besides, you're walking on eggshells when you deal with a writer, because they tend to be flaky. But I reminded him of how I'd demonstrated an understanding of his needs, and more to the point, I'd made him money. Then I got out my list of best buys, and since I knew that now he was much more financially secure and that he did have a bit of the gambler's mentality, I threw in a few somewhat volatile stocks among my recommendations. In the end he decided to continue with my firm, and by and large, the portfolio I recommended continued to earn him an excellent rate of return."

"That was lucky," Fred agreed supportively. "But I imagine you have had the occasional disappointment," he continued.

"I had a big one," Mort said. "I was selling a complicated group plan to the executive of a major corporation. Frankly, I was out of my league, and I failed. I took it hard; I just wasn't used to losing."

"What did you do to get over the disappointment?" Fred asked.

"I was so disheartened that I didn't come into the office for nearly a week," Mort said. "After that, I decided I would never try to sell a group policy again. But I also learned to accept that sometimes people simply won't buy. Maybe they are convinced they don't need the product, it's not right for them, they can't afford it, or whatever. Nowadays I don't take it personally."

As Fred jotted a note, Mort went on. "I had an instance that was similar to the case of the author. An eminent physician had received a large amount of money from selling a patent and called me for my recommendations. I knew he was well versed in financial matters, and I was flattered that he asked for advice from me. Yet when I presented my alternatives, he seemed to resent my counsel."

"But you landed the account?" Fred immediately rephrased the leading question. "What happened?"

"I didn't get the business. I figure that, for some reason, he just didn't take to me, which happens," Mort replied. "I did track the stocks I recommended compared to those the physician purchased through another firm, and my choices performed slightly better. That took some of the sting out of the lost sale."

Fred progressed to his other dimensions. After he thanked Mort and escorted him out, Fred and Jimmy rendezvoused with Mack the Hack, who was waiting in front of the UnitedCo building as Jimmy had previously arranged.

"City Athletic Club," Jimmy told Mack. "And don't spare the horses."

Mack pulled out into traffic. "Speaking of horses . . ." he began, launching into a series of "hot tips" on that day's card at City Downs.

Jimmy stifled the urge to reach for his wallet. While he could feel the two-spots burning a hole in his pocket, somehow his gambling urge was less compelling.

CHAPTER TWENTY-TWO

Are you planning on taking in the Annual City Disabled Tennis Tournament?" Mack the Hack asked.

"Whaddaya know about it?" Jimmy demanded.

Mack glanced in the rearview mirror. "Most of the participants use wheelchairs, and you'll be impressed at how well they cover the court. Last year in the men's finals, Rackets O'Reilly came from the baseline to the net for a put-away that won the match. His mom was in the stands, and by the way, she makes a heck of a corned beef and cabbage. Her secret is slow simmering. Did I mention that over the stove she's got a print of Dali's *Persistence of Vision*?"

◄

"Enough already," Jimmy protested. "Sheesh! Why is it everyone but me knows all this stuff?"

At the tennis facility, Jimmy and Fred took a table in the clubhouse restaurant and watched through large glass windows as Jennifer competed in the semifinals of the women's singles event. According to the scoreboard, she'd won the first set and was leading 5–3 in the second.

Paula arrived from her dentist appointment. "Any cavities?" Jimmy asked.

"No, but I've got to remember to floss regularly," she said. Outside on the court, Jennifer hit a wicked backhand that passed her opponent. Jennifer played an aggressive game. She charged the net frequently and went for the "kill" shot rather than waiting for the other player to make an unforced error. Although she double-faulted fairly often, the serves that did go in were almost always winners.

The scoreboard lit up with the results of the match. Jennifer was victorious, two sets to none.

A few minutes later she joined them in the clubhouse. "Thanks for meeting with me here," she said. "I was really looking forward to this tournament."

"Congratulations on winning your match," Paula said. "Are you also entered in the doubles event?"

"Doubles is popular in our league," Jennifer responded, "but I prefer singles. I like to make it on my own."

A waiter brought tea as Paula began the interview. In

response to her first question regarding a particularly rewarding experience as a librarian, Jennifer said, "I was working at the reference desk, and the winter-sports columnist for the local newspaper came in and asked why people get goose bumps. I came up empty-handed after checking encyclopedias and medical texts, but I got a hunch, consulted a book on evolution, and found the answer."

Jimmy couldn't overcome his curiosity. "Why do we get goose bumps?"

"It's a throwback," Jennifer replied. "For protection against the cold, tiny arrectores pilorum muscles at the base of body hair try to fluff up our pelt to make a thicker, more insulating, air-bearing coat—except humans no longer have pelts. I found that fascinating, and so did the columnist. When he ran the item, he gave me a prominent acknowledgment for my research assistance."

"That was a nice compliment," Paula said. "But soon after that you gave up library work."

"I was reassigned to check out books, and often there were long periods between patrons," Jennifer said. "I'd enjoyed my work at the reference desk, so I occupied my free time by helping out the reference desk staff by taking inquiries there. I felt I was performing a service, but once in a while people had to wait at the front counter, and some complained. The library director ordered me to stay at my post, which was a shame. I was doing the work of two people."

Jennifer sipped her tea. "At that point, I reevaluated my situation. I'd studied library science because my college advisor thought it was a suitable profession for a person using a wheelchair, but I decided I could do more. I like helping people, being active, getting recognition for work well done, and frankly, I'm aware that I have a psychological need to demonstrate that my disability doesn't mean I can't compete and succeed in the workforce. In analyzing my strengths, I decided that sales was a profession I could excel in."

"It appears that you have," Paula said.

"Thank you," Jennifer said. "It's been an enlightening experience. My first position was with a company that consolidated book purchases from small libraries so they could obtain group discounts. I made plenty of sales, but all were rather small because my clients were small and their purchases were dictated by budget allocations. I felt my abilities were underutilized. I wanted the chance at larger orders and the rewards that come with them. I found it when I successfully applied to City Information Services."

"Can you tell me a bit about the job?"

"I represent integrated custom software for financial institutions," Jennifer said. "It gives me the opportunity for major sales, since our programs are priced from $500,000 to well over a million in the case of larger banks. Naturally, the sales cycle is relatively long, requiring a great deal of vertically integrated contact with many of the clients' departments, from IS right down to the tellers and auditors who are the end users. Our proposals have to address everyone's needs, including such details as the most useful design for screen displays."

"Tell me about a sale you are particularly proud of," Paula said.

"One client was a small, family-held bank with a 100-year tradition, and the decision maker was the president. Unfortunately, I was having a devil of a time getting to meet with him because he'd assigned his systems manager to deal with me. And it became obvious she was deliberately obstructing my access to her boss, perhaps because she felt her own position was threatened by the purchase of my software."

Jennifer smiled at the recollection. "I got a brainstorm. I researched thoroughly—my library training came in handy—then wrote a newspaper-style story about the bank, dated five years in the future. I had it printed as a feature article on a mock-up of a *Wall Street Journal* front page. After detailing the bank's proud history, the article reported how the company had doubled its assets and reduced its costs by using my software. I sent it to the president, and the next day he phoned and asked me to come in. In the end I placed my software and earned a big commission."

"That was an innovative approach." Paula jotted a note. "But now you are considering moving on to UnitedCo."

"Recently my company announced a faster and much more comprehensive software program," Jennifer explained.

"I reviewed its specs and sold it to a major client."

But Jennifer did not look pleased. "It turned out to be 'vaporware,'" she went on, "and having already instituted procedural changes in anticipation of it, the client lost a good deal of time and money. Our programmers took forever to get their act together, and frankly, I'm surprised they weren't fired, since they cost us several lucrative clients."

The waiter refilled their teacups. "I like working as a member of a team," Jennifer said, "but I expect my teammates to stay up to speed. So I'm seeking a position with more opportunity for sales, and less dependence on things I have no control over."

Paula turned the conversation to Planning and Organizing.

"My disability does put demands on my time," Jennifer said, "so I've always carefully scheduled my day. Whenever possible, I slate a midday appointment with a client located near the restaurant district so I can eat lunch without having to reboard my specially-equipped vehicle."

The public address system called Jennifer to the court for her finals match. Paula wished her well in the tournament.

To Jimmy's relief, they decided to take lunch in the Clubhouse. He figured a ritzy joint like this would at least have something on the menu more toothsome than mystery meat.

CHAPTER TWENTY-THREE

"**B**oy, Jennifer is a piece of work," Jimmy said as their meals were served.

"What are you talking about, Kid?" Paula asked.

"Am I the only member of this troika that she struck as single-minded?" asked Jimmy rhetorically. "Everything with her is about making the big kill, and when she doesn't, it's someone else's fault."

"But look at the bottom line," Fred said. "Jennifer has made the big kill, and repeatedly."

Jimmy paused dramatically. "How?"

"What are you driving at, Kid?" Paula asked.

"I'm not saying that this notion of yours that past behavior predicts future behavior isn't spot-on," Jimmy said, "but wouldn't it help if we could actually observe how our suspects behave?"

"That would be a useful supplement to the information we have on the critical dimensions," Fred agreed. "How should we do it?"

Jimmy smiled. "Did you ever read that scene near the end of *The Big Sleep*, where Philip Marlowe thinks that Carmen Sternwood is the killer, but he can't be positive, so he takes her target shooting?"

Fred excitedly took up the thread. "While Marlowe is setting up the targets, she fires the gun at him five times."

"Marlowe has loaded it with blanks," Paula continued. "But it shows that she has the capacity to commit homicide."

"Aha!" Jimmy pointed accusing fingers at Fred and Paula. "So you two read detective novels too!"

"Once in a rare while," Fred admitted.

"Now and then," Paula confessed.

"I see where you're leading, Jimmy," Fred said, "but I'm way ahead of you. For example, I like to test a candidate's Sales Ability by asking him to sell me a pencil."

"But UnitedCo's products are a lot more sophisticated than pencils, Fred," Jimmy noted. "Why not have the candidates sell one of your actual products?"

Fred nodded judiciously. "That's certainly better than the pencil test, but it would give an advantage to a person with prior experience in our field. Besides, our products are quite complex. Instead, why don't we choose a hypothetical product that's not so complicated but requires the same selling skills?"

Fred was making notes now. "It strikes me that when this sales simulation is completed, it should form a complete STAR. I'll start by providing the Situation. The Task, of course, is to make a sale. And the applicant provides the Action, which determines the Result."

All three pitched in to "invent" the product, an innovative computerized control device costing about $40,000. They listed its accuracy, reliability, and uses, all of which were favorable, because there was little point in setting the candidates up for failure by making the product inferior. They chose PJF as the company name.

Next they created the client, Ralph O'Hara, a senior vice president for a manufacturing company with three plants around the country. Ralph, who had not previously purchased from PJF, requested more information about the device after seeing an advertisement in a magazine specializing in business technology. After a preliminary phone conversation, a sales call had been set up.

The background information on the product and on Ralph would be presented in written form to each candidate. Realizing that to be fair, they must set time limits for assimilating the information and making the sales presentation, they decided on 20 minutes and 15 minutes, respectively.

"Since I'm most experienced in sales, should I play the role of Ralph?" Fred suggested. They agreed, and Paula and Jimmy helped him develop standard answers to issues and questions that might be brought up, such as problems with present equipment and anticipated changes in operations.

"In a meeting like this, would Ralph be likely to raise objections?" Paula asked.

"That's a good point," Fred replied. They added a half dozen, including expense, management's resistance to change, and an inquiry on error rate. With each candidate, Fred would bring up at least two of these points. Lastly, they decided that if the discussion wasn't over in 14 minutes, Fred would say he had another appointment and had to leave in one minute. That would give them a chance to see what sort of close and follow-up the candidate would suggest.

"So the best result won't be a done deal," Jimmy said. "That makes sense. A manager isn't about to commit to such a large purchase after a 15-minute presentation, and our candidates are smart enough to know that."

"Correct," Fred said. "A positive result would be that the candidate shows Ralph that the product has strong potential for him, and a second appointment is made to discuss the product with some of the other managers in the company."

Looking at his notebook, Fred said, "In other words, Paula, a simulation is a supplement to other interviews. It provides additional behavioral information that is, by the very nature of the simulation, highly relevant to the job."

"Yes," Paula said, "and it's another important part of our Targeted Solution system."

TARGETED SOLUTION #6:
SUPPLEMENT INTERVIEW
INFORMATION WITH OBSERVATIONS
FROM BEHAVIORAL SIMULATIONS.

• Simulations allow a candidate to demonstrate skills.

• Well-devised simulations are fair to all candidates, whatever their prior experience in the work area.

Fred looked up from his notebook with concern. "But when will we administer the simulations? Tomorrow is Saturday." Fred was crestfallen. "I was truly hoping to make my job offer first thing Monday morning."

"I took the liberty of arranging follow-up appointments with each of our four candidates over the weekend," Paula stated.

Fred and Jimmy gaped at Paula. "So you already knew we'd need simulations," Jimmy said.

"I'm supposed to know these things," Paula kidded. "I'm a professionally trained detective. Seriously, I was confident that you two would detect on your own the value of Targeted Simulations for supplementing interview data."

"Speaking of detection," Fred said, "what about The Faker?"

"Yeah," Jimmy chimed in. "Even with the simulations, if the culprit is as good as he or she appears to be, how do we know that we won't be fooled after all?"

"We've got all this data," Fred added, "but what do we do with it?"

Paula showed them her Cheshire cat grin. "The last simulation appointment is early Sunday afternoon. After that, can you both be at my apartment at four o'clock?"

Fred gave Paula a steady gaze. "Tell the truth, Paula," he said. "Do you know who The Faker is?"

"No," Paula said honestly, "but I do know this: Before Monday morning we'll uncover not only The Faker, but the person who will do the top-notch job for UnitedCo."

CHAPTER TWENTY-FOUR

Mack the Hack dropped Paula and Jimmy off at the detective agency, and Fred felt distinct confidence when he bid them adieu. It looked as if there was an increasingly better chance that they would, after all, solve this . . .

". . . mystery." Mack's voice interrupted Fred's thought.

"I beg your pardon, Mack?"

"I just asked if you were a fan of the mystery," Mack said, "because Biff Jones is making an appearance at City Books this evening at six to autograph his latest opus. It's called *Death Comes A-knocking*."

"Waddaya know about it?" Fred demanded.

Mack gave him a sharp look in the rearview mirror. "Hey, that's Jimmy's line."

"I was just kidding, Mack. As a matter of fact, I've read two of Biff's previous books, and I enjoyed them quite a bit."

"Well, in this one, it turns out that the real murderer is . . ."

"Mack!" Fred said sharply.

"Sorry." Mack contritely let Fred off at the front door of the UnitedCo building.

After a long afternoon of catching up on work that had piled up on his desk during the investigation of The Case of The Faker, Fred remembered what Mack had told him about Biff Jones' book signing. City Books was only a few blocks away, so Fred decided to stop by before heading for home. He relished the chance to meet one of his favorite authors.

As he entered the bookstore, Fred saw a table to one side on which were piles of the new Biff Jones book. They were so tall that they formed an almost jail-bar-like barrier enclosing a slight, middle-aged, bespectacled, balding store clerk. Assuming he was early, Fred nodded pleasantly at the clerk, took a book from the top of one pile, and leafed through it at random. Even by merely skimming it, Fred could see it was chock-full of the two-fisted, hard-boiled, tough-guy prose that was Biff Jones' trademark. Fred guessed that Jones himself would be, to use one of Jimmy's terms, "a tough mug."

Fred's eye fell on the author's biography at the back of the book. After writing several critically acclaimed novels that sold poorly, Biff struck gold when a producer came across one of the novels, *The Deadly Damsel*, and paid a large sum for movie rights. The movie was a big hit, and as a result, Biff received a very generous advance for his next book, which was a best-seller. After the movie sale, Biff had . . .

Fred closed the book in surprise. Something about Biff's story struck a strongly familiar note.

He approached the clerk. "Excuse me," Fred said, "but will Biff be here soon?"

The mild-mannered "clerk" smiled. "I'm Biff Jones." He shook his head. "Geez, I wish to heck people would show up for these darned things. It's the hardest way in the world to sell books."

Thinking fast, Fred said, "I was hoping you'd sign one for me, and two more for some friends." Fred told Biff his name, and asked him to inscribe the other two for Jimmy and Paula.

Biff brightened a bit and went to work signing the books. As he finished, Fred said, "I believe you may know an acquaintance of mine. His name is Mort Saroyan."

For a moment, Fred was distressed at his own directness. He feared that Biff would ask how Fred had come to this conclusion.

Instead, Biff seemed instantly preoccupied with some thought the query had triggered—and it clearly wasn't a pleasant recollection. "Are you a friend of Mort's?" he asked instead.

"I wouldn't say a friend, exactly," Fred replied carefully. "Mort handled a one-time sale of a small amount of stock I inherited."

Biff slid the three books across the table toward Fred. "Then I suppose you didn't suffer from Mort's counsel— and I wish I could say the same."

"What happened?"

"I engaged Mort as my investment advisor after I made my first big sale, but I had to let him go. The return he was obtaining was chicken feed compared to what some of my friends were getting. I was losing money. I dropped him three months ago, like a nervous barber drops a hot towel."

"That's a swell metaphor, Biff."

Fred heard a commotion behind him. A gaggle of book fans had finally arrived, and Biff perked up considerably. Having made his sale to Fred and seeing the customers at Fred's back, Biff looked at him pointedly and said, "Next."

Fred paid for his books and headed home. As soon as he arrived, he dialed Paula's office number and found her and Jimmy still there. He asked Paula to put him on speaker, and then he related his experience at the bookstore.

"Wow!" Jimmy said. "It sounds like Mort told us a whopper."

"What do you think we should do?" Paula asked, her tone more reassuringly calm.

Fred reviewed his recent experience. "I'd better ponder on that," he replied.

CHAPTER TWENTY-FIVE

Two evenings later, Fred helped Paula clear the table after an early supper that she'd prepared—pasta with puttanesca sauce, accompanied by baby asparagus. Fred volunteered to wash if Jimmy dried.

Jimmy had never been in Paula's apartment before. The kitchen was neat and airy, with a view of the river, which Jimmy might have enjoyed if he hadn't been so impatient to get to the solution of the case. As soon as they finished with the dishes, they rejoined Paula at the table and pulled out their notes.

"Fred, the other day you asked how we deal with all the data we've obtained," Paula began.

"That's the final part of my Targeted Solution system. To uncover both The Faker and Fred's new salesperson, we must share the information we separately obtained and integrate that data in an organized way."

Paula suggested that to begin, they each go over their interview notes to evaluate the STARs they'd obtained.

"How would we do that?" Jimmy asked.

"I'd suggest that we review our STARs," Fred said, "first to make certain none are incomplete or theoretical, and second, to determine the dimension each goes under."

"I thought we did that," Jimmy protested. "I mean, when you get a STAR by asking 'How do you plan your week?' obviously it goes under Planning and Organizing."

"Nonetheless," Fred said, "when I reread my notes this morning, it seemed that some of the STARs I obtained while asking about one dimension actually demonstrated key actions of another."

Jimmy could see Fred's point, and he checked his own notes. "As a matter of fact," he said, "I got a story from Mort while I was looking into Motivation Fit, but I have a nagging feeling it should go somewhere else."

"What was the story?" asked Fred.

"As a boy, Mort sought a part-time job to earn money to go to summer camp," Jimmy said. "Several neighbors who were senior citizens had their groceries delivered, and Mort thought that might be a service he could provide for a more attractive fee. Looking into the situation, he learned that the only shop that delivered was an expensive corner store that added a $5 surcharge. Mort offered to fill orders at a chain supermarket and deliver for only $3. He lined up several prospective clients and got a loan from his father to buy carrying baskets to install on his bike and to print up some fliers describing his service. He exceeded his sales and profit projections and enjoyed the exercise and the company of the older folks."

"What dimension did you see that behavior falling under?" queried Fred.

"While there's a hint of Motivation in the story, I thought it related more to Analysis," Jimmy said. "Mort identified the issues and got all the necessary information. According to our definition, that sounds like Analysis to me. Then he took the initiative to implement his ideas. I might have gotten some information on Sales Ability also, but I didn't really pursue that. I know the result but don't know how he actually did it."

"That's astute, Kid," Paula said. "A good way to correctly classify a STAR is by comparing it to the definition of the dimension and its key actions."

"What's next?" Jimmy asked.

"Each of us will evaluate the STARs we've obtained. I suggest that we use a 5-point rating scale. Here's one I've employed over the years." Paula pulled a piece of paper from her briefcase and showed it to Fred and Jimmy.

5 = Much More Than Acceptable

4 = More Than Acceptable

3 = Acceptable

2 = Less Than Acceptable

1 = Much Less Than Acceptable

"Got any recommendations on assigning the ratings?" Jimmy questioned.

"As a matter of fact, I do," Paula replied. "First, for each dimension, we must determine whether the STARs, as viewed overall, represent positive or negative behaviors. A person might have three positive STARs in Planning and Organizing, and one STAR that is negative. At first glance this might seem to indicate that the candidate is satisfactory, but not perfect, in the dimension."

"But what if the negative STAR was fairly irrelevant to Fred's sales representative position?" Jimmy said. "For example, a candidate's three positive STARs involve recent solutions to planning her day, but she also tells you about the time she lost all of her orders while selling Girl Scout Cookies when she was 12. I don't think I'd give that a lot of weight if the positive STARs indicated that a lesson was learned."

"Conversely, that's similar to the story you related about Mort's grocery-delivery business," Fred said. "While it's positive in several dimensions, as we discussed, it doesn't relate strongly, in recency or relevancy, to selling UnitedCo's sort of products. So I'd tend to give it less weight."

Jimmy turned to Paula. "I think I'm getting a handle on your 1-to-5 rating scale. But, for Fred's job opening, do we want to consider only the people whose consensus ratings are mostly 4s or 5s?"

Fred provided the answer. "Only if we had superhuman applicants. Remember, these ratings aren't like grades in grammar school. A 3 means acceptable. In our situation it would mean they consistently meet sales goals."

"Boy, that seems like a system that will work." But Jimmy noticed that Fred's expression was clouded.

"Paula, assuming that your system ferrets out The Faker," Fred said, "we'll still be left with three potential candidates. What if none of them is clearly predicted to succeed, based on past behaviors?"

Jimmy was impatient to solve the mystery. "We just pick the best of the lot."

Fred stared at him for quite a while. "You've hit on something, Jimmy."

"Well, it's pretty obvious."

"No, I meant that you're wrong." Fred saw Jimmy's jaw drop, and quickly added, "No offense intended. You see, that's exactly the mistake I made with Richard Bronson, Joe Jackson's predecessor, who lasted only 18 months in the Central District position. He was the best of the lot— but it wasn't a very good lot."

"Still, like now, you're supposed to hire someone," Jimmy said.

"Just as we are supposed to find the guilty party when we take on a mystery," Paula said. "But how long do you think we'd last in the detective business if we accused innocent people?"

"Exactly the mistake I made, Paula," Fred said. "I was under pressure to hire, so I chose the candidate who was 'better' than the others. But that didn't mean he was qualified."

"So you're saying that if you don't meet your hiring deadline, you might lose some money in the short run," Jimmy restated. "But if you hire an unqualified candidate, you definitely lose more money in the end. That means that when the search for the perpetrator doesn't reveal the culprit, we continue the search."

"It really is a lot like detective work," Fred said. "We need to depend solely on evidence—and our evidence is the STARs."

CHAPTER TWENTY-SIX

The shadows slanting through the windows of Paula's kitchen lengthened as the three members of the team completed their ratings.

In the corner of the room, Paula had set up an easel with a large pad similar to the one in Fred's office. She tore off the first four pages and posted them on the wall. Each sheet had a candidate's name on it and a grid on which the investigators could post their ratings.

"I'm not sure I'm clear on how we come to a consensus. Do the two people who interviewed the candidate on a dimension vote?" Fred asked a little anxiously. "Or do we add up the numbers and work out an average?"

◄

Mort Saroyan	Fred	Paula	Jimmy	Consen.
Persuasiveness/ Sales Ability				
Resilience				
Analysis				
Planning and Organizing				
Judgment				
Initiative				
Motivational Fit				
Oral Communication				
Impact				

"Neither one," Paula replied. "Let me give you an example. Assume that Jimmy gives a candidate a 4 in Resilience, and I give a 3. At that point we'd share the STARs that led each of us to our ratings. This could produce any one of a number of results."

"I'm getting a glimmer of what you mean," Jimmy said. "It could turn out that my examples aren't really as strong as I first thought, or that they are undercut somewhat when compared to yours. That would convince me to agree with your 3."

"Or," Fred said, "your examples were strong, while in our discussion we realized that Paula's, while slightly less positive, also were less recent or less relevant to the job. In that case your 4 would stand."

"It's even possible," Paula added, "that, in 'comparing notes,' we'd decide that contradictory data revealed the candidate as less resilient than either of us thought at first, and we'd choose a 2 as the most accurate consensus."

"That's a relief," Jimmy said. "I was never that good in math anyway."

Paula suggested that they begin with Mort.

"Why bother?" Jimmy questioned. "Remember, one drop of ink taints the whole glass of milk."

"I'm not sure I understand your metaphor, Jimmy," Fred said.

"Mort lied to us once. That makes everything he's told us a possible skein of deception."

"True," Paula said, "assuming that he lied." She smiled at Fred.

"Do you two have some secret I should be in on?" Jimmy asked irritably.

"When I told you of Biff's story about how Mort had not done a good job for him," Fred said to Paula, "you suggested that something should be done about it. Once again you were pointing me in a direction, and eventually I realized what it was."

"I bet a two-spot I know," Jimmy said. "You gave Mort a chance to tell his side of the story."

Fred nodded. "I met with him this morning. To my surprise, when I told him of my encounter with Biff, he did not seem like someone 'caught in the act,' but merely appeared a bit saddened."

Fred referred to his notebook. "I jotted down the rest of the conversation in detail, and I can relate it almost verbatim. That might help you evaluate who the liar is.

"Mort began, 'I'm not a psychologist, Fred, so I can't explain why Biff would have told you what he did. But I can make a guess. As I've said, Biff was always looking for the same big win in his investments that he'd achieved in his writing. As he became more wealthy, this desire became greater. Additionally, Biff is by profession a romancer, and he also has quite an ego. He's the type capable of making up a tale—and even believing it's true—as a way of denying that he'd made a mistake or was responsible for a poor result.'

"'Then you are asserting that he did make up a tale,' I said.

"'Biff did take his account to another brokerage,' Mort said. 'I didn't mention this to you because a client-broker relationship is rarely a marriage for life. Clients leave all the time. I didn't think it was significant.'

"'It's certainly significant if he had a good cause,' I said.

"'Maybe in his mind he did,' Mort replied. 'Did he lose money, as he claimed? Yes, if you call a one-point-in-time drop in value of 3 or 4 stocks out of a 20-stock portfolio losing money. So what? No investment advisor is right every time. The bottom line is this: During the time I worked with Biff, there was no extended period of time when the overall value of his holdings did not appreciate. Further, over the long term, his average gain was a bit higher than the market average.'

"'You referred to a mistake Biff made,' I said.

"'His mistake was being an impossible client,' Mort amplified. 'Some time after Biff left my firm, I met a colleague from another brokerage who confided that Biff was now his client. My colleague was beside himself because Biff kept demanding investments he heard about from his movie friends, and then blaming him when they went sour. It was all my colleague could do to maintain even a minimal appreciation in Biff's account.'

"Mort could see that I'd be happier with proof and that I was uncomfortable asking for it," Fred told Jimmy and Paula. "So he provided it. He said, 'All of my trades on Biff's behalf—and their results—are a matter of written record, of course. While I can't show them to you for reasons of client confidentiality, I can show them to my manager, and he can confirm in a general way that all the numbers I've given you are true. Feel free to call him. He knows I'm looking for another position.'"

Fred looked up at Paula and Jimmy. "I did so, and the conversation was brief. Mort's supervisor attested to the results Mort claimed, and he volunteered that they were consistent with Mort's excellent performance for his entire slate of clients."

"So we've got two possibilities," Jimmy said. "Number one is that Biff Jones is a savvy investor who was grievously victimized by Mort, who then falsified records and entered into a conspiracy with his manager to cover up. Number two is that Mort is completely innocent of the charges leveled by Biff."

Paula smiled. "I think we've answered that one beyond a reasonable doubt. Shall we get to work?"

They did, turning their attention to the grid on which Mort's ratings had been posted.

"Fred, you rated Mort significantly higher on Sales Ability than I did," Paula began.

"I gave a lot of weight to his overall career." Fred pointed out that Mort had successfully sold increasingly sophisticated products, moving from books to insurance to stocks. Fred also detailed STARs that showed how Mort refined his skills with each new position. "That would seem to strongly argue that Mort will be up to the greater challenge of working for UnitedCo," Fred concluded.

Paula also had data showing sales successes, but she reminded Fred that they also had several STARs about sales that Mort failed to make. She suggested that Mort's admitted failure with many clients raised the question of whether his success might be more a function of the number of clients rather than the quality of selling. "Do you think that might be an issue with regard to your position?" she asked.

"You do have a point," Fred conceded. "My 4 is a bit high. I'd say Mort is more in the satisfactory range."

"How would you feel about a 3?" Paula suggested. Fred agreed, and Paula entered that rating in the consensus column.

Mort Saroyan	Fred	Paula	Jimmy	Consen.
Persuasiveness/ Sales Ability	4	2		
Resilience	4		2	
Analysis		3	2	
Planning and Organizing		3	2	
Judgment	3		3	
Initiative	3	3		
Motivational Fit	4	4		
Oral Communication	3	3	3	
Impact	3	4	4	

For Resilience Jimmy defended his 2 rating with the STAR about how badly Mort took it when he failed to make the big group insurance sale. Fred argued that the STAR could be viewed as positive, because from the experience, Mort learned how to accept the inevitable rejections that are a part of sales. In addition, Mort's willingness to pursue so many leads despite their relatively high failure rate was arguably a negative in Sales Ability, but it seemed a strong plus in Resilience.

Jimmy agreed with Fred's rating of 4 in that dimension, and they turned their attention to those that remained. As they finished coming to consensus on Mort's ratings, Paula put on the tea kettle.

Next, they looked at Millicent's ratings. In Judgment Fred had given her a 2, while Jimmy's rating was a 4.

"Jimmy, you do have many STARs showing that Millicent is creative and makes logical decisions based on factual information," Fred said. "But I have one that shows abysmal judgment. While serving on The City Homeless Project's annual fund-raiser subcommittee, Millicent proposed an auction of the sort that had been profitable in the past. Another member, named Jane, was adamant they hold a masked ball. For inexplicable reasons, Millicent agreed, even though she knew it would be a financial disaster—and it was. Because of Millicent's poor decision, the organization actually lost money."

Fred looked up to find Jimmy smiling smugly. "There's more to it, Fred," he said. "I got the rest of the story when

I asked Millicent if she'd ever resorted to subterfuge, since I figured her for The Faker."

Jimmy considered. "Maybe she's not, but never mind. You see, another result was that Jane got the blame for the masked ball flopping and resigned from the committee. That was Millicent's plan all along, because this Jane had a personality disorder and, as treasurer of the Project, was embezzling funds. So Millicent had to get rid of her."

"That still seems like poor judgment," Fred insisted. "Millicent stopped the monetary drain, but only by losing more money."

Jimmy shook his head. "Even though Millicent was certain she was stealing, Jane was influential, Millicent didn't have hard evidence, and besides, Millicent liked Jane and didn't want to expose her publicly. After Jane's ouster, Millicent went to her, convinced her that she had Jane's best interests in mind, and Jane agreed to seek treatment for her condition."

"Millicent still had a fiduciary duty to her organization," Fred said stubbornly.

"I'm like the Royal Canadian Mounties," Jimmy declared. "I always get my man . . . er, STAR . . . and here's the ultimate result. Once Jane's disability was controlled with medication, she was fraught with remorse and wanted to turn herself in. Instead, Millicent suggested that Jane make a contribution to the Project that more than covered both her thefts and the loss on the masked ball. And that's not even the end of it—now

Millicent and Jane are close friends."

"Wow," Fred said. "I wouldn't have known the whole story—or STAR—in a million years if we hadn't integrated our data."

As he began to write in his notebook, Fred said, "Jimmy, would you mind entering a 4 in Judgment for Millicent. I want to get this thought down while it's fresh in my mind."

"Sure, Fred."

"I understood what we were doing in discussing our STARs," Fred said as he wrote, "but now I see why it works—for example, to give us the full story about Millicent. And," he added, flourishing his notebook, "I believe it has pointed me to the final component of our system."

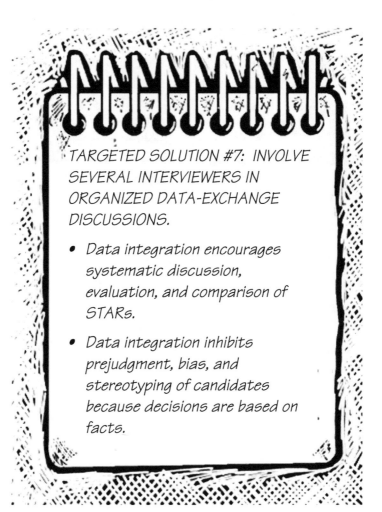

TARGETED SOLUTION #7: INVOLVE SEVERAL INTERVIEWERS IN ORGANIZED DATA-EXCHANGE DISCUSSIONS.

- *Data integration encourages systematic discussion, evaluation, and comparison of STARs.*

- *Data integration inhibits prejudgment, bias, and stereotyping of candidates because decisions are based on facts.*

CHAPTER TWENTY-SEVEN

Paula asked Jimmy to lead the discussion on Jennifer and post the ratings. They were all 4s and 3s.

"I'll be a hog-tied heifer!" Jimmy said. "It looks like you have your top candidate, Fred."

"Before we jump to conclusions, Kid, let's go on with the integration process," Paula said. "Fred, while both of you rated Jennifer strong in Judgment, you scored her a 4 and the Kid gave her a 5."

"I had several positive STARs," Fred said, "but one that was negative. In her present position, Jennifer decided to take Friday afternoons off. She felt that it wouldn't be a problem because that was the period set aside for paperwork that had to be turned in at the top of the week, which she could do on her own time over the weekend. But one Friday a client needed to place a large emergency order and was unable to reach her because the battery in her pager died. That cost a sale."

"That could happen to anyone," Jimmy said, with some exasperation.

"True," Fred said, "but the proportion of good judgments to bad doesn't equal a 5 for Jennifer in my book."

"Maybe I was too positive overall with Jennifer," Jimmy replied. "I felt badly about the unfair questions I asked the first time I spoke with her. In my second interview I was impressed with her sales successes, and I gave that a lot of weight."

Jimmy checked his notes. "I guess I let how she got around her disability affect my reaction to her, but that's no more valid than making assumptions because someone wears glasses or is short or tall."

Jimmy marked down the consensus rating of 4 for Jennifer in Judgment, and with the discussion continuing, the three of them came to a consensus on the other dimensions. Jennifer's ratings remained the highest of any candidate so far, and in most dimensions her strengths were rated as more than satisfactory.

For the first time during this busy week, Fred felt as if the weight of the world was not on his shoulders. Jennifer was clearly a skilled salesperson, and Thomas Goldman's evaluation was still to come. In one or the other, he had his new representative.

His elation lasted all of three seconds.

Both of them were good—and as they already knew, so was The Faker. Fred felt like the fellow in the story *The Lady or the Tiger*: Behind one door was the person who would keep Central District tops in sales; behind the other was the person with the potential to drag it down— and Fred as well.

Putting aside his uneasy feeling, Fred joined in as they looked at Thomas' ratings. The discussion moved rapidly until they got to Planning and Organizing.

"I had some trouble getting STARs in this dimension," Paula admitted. "I asked Thomas several questions about how he arranged a typical sales week, but I couldn't pin him down. While I got no negative examples, the overall impression was that he didn't feel this area was important. Because our Job Analysis indicates it is, I gave him a 2."

"In contrast, I got several specific STARs that support my 3," Jimmy offered. "Thomas helped his regional manager organize and execute a plan for hiring several salespeople, and all of them worked out. When a supplier was late with an important component, he figured out a way that customers could be serviced with minimum delay. He was instrumental in devising a marketing strategy for a new product, and another time, he developed an effective schedule for the changeover to a new billing procedure."

"Good work, Kid," Paula said. "Based on what you've told us, I agree that Thomas rates a 3. Let's also talk about some of those examples when we get to Initiative. They go beyond some of the data I got. Fred, how do you feel about a 3 in Planning and Organizing?"

"Looks good to me," Fred responded. And they posted the consensus rating.

After further discussion, they completed their integration of data on Thomas. Now Paula entered the consensus ratings for all the candidates on another grid.

	Mort	Jen	Milli	Thomas
Persuasiveness/ Sales Ability	3	4	2	4
Resilience	4	4	3	3
Analysis	3	4	4	4
Planning and Organizing	3	3	4	3
Judgment	3	4	4	4
Initiative	3	4	4	4
Motivational Fit	4	4	1	4
Oral Communication	3	3	4	5
Impact	3	3	4	4

CHAPTER TWENTY-EIGHT

P aula set a plate on the table. "Hot dog!" Jimmy said. "There's nothing I like better than chocolate cake."

"It's carob-frosted zucchini bread," Paula said.

Jimmy paused in mid chew. "Aw heck, Paula," he protested, "what kind of dessert has vegetables in it?" He continued to chew. "Good, though," he conceded.

Fred had been doing some quick math in his notebook. "If you add up the ratings, Jennifer and Thomas are virtually tied for best candidate, as are Mort and Millicent for less satisfactory candidate. However, all four have an average rating of . . ."

"Excuse me, Fred," Paula gently interrupted, "but I don't really think we'll learn much about candidate success by treating the ratings as if they are sports scores."

Fred looked up from his figures. "I tend to be the statistical sort," he said, "but I see your point."

"Instead of looking at this as a numbers game," Paula said, "let's see what each person's dimensional ratings mean relative to each other. For example, a candidate who is poor in the dimension of Judgment but very high in Initiative could pose a big problem."

"Especially if the job the candidate was applying for was decision maker at a nuclear missile site," Jimmy said. "In that situation I'd sure as heck want a manager whose initiative was well tempered by judgment."

"It might not be quite that obvious," Paula said, smiling, "but I'm certain that all the clues we need are in the data we've obtained. We've just got to work harder to dig them out. For example, we haven't considered your ratings on the simulations, Fred. Tell us about them."

"Starting with Mort, essentially, he failed to sell me," Fred said. "He began by looking to my needs, but there was no customization of his sales presentation. Mort wasn't approaching me as a specific customer for a specific product, but as a generic 'prospect.' I felt he was merely using one of the patterned presentations he'd developed over his sales career."

Fred consulted his notes. "Even though he took all the allotted time to prepare, Mort did not seem to comprehend the product very well, as if he was 'in over his head.' I was clear on the benefits my organization expected from the product, but Mort didn't go after them."

Fred turned the page. "The biggest problem, though, was that he didn't seem to know how to close. When I tossed out the old diversionary tactic of saying, 'I'll take this up with my management committee,' he thanked me and left. A more appropriate and effective step would have been to offer to present to the committee himself, or to make a member of his technical team available to answer further questions, or even to ask if he could check in with me in the future."

Fred looked perplexed. "Mort has a fine sales record— so why couldn't he get me to say 'yes'?"

A clue to the answer was tickling at the back of Jimmy's mind, and it had to do with a term that Paula had used a few minutes earlier. "Numbers game!" he exclaimed.

Paula and Fred looked at him. "That's the same way Mort described sales," Jimmy explained, "and there are all sorts of echoes of it in the stories he gave us."

Fred saw what Jimmy meant. "We've discussed how Mort succeeded more on volume of sales calls than quality of presentation," he said, "and that corresponds to his performance in the simulation. Mort has always depended on lists and 'scripts.' When something worked once with a particular customer—such as comparing his books to the competitors'—he added it to his repertoire on the assumption that it would work with all of his other customers. When he recommended investments, he did it from two generic 'menus,' one listing the products and the other listing a typical client's needs. He used a 'mix and match' approach, although granted, it resulted in many sales."

"But now we're back to statistics," Jimmy said. "Mort's method succeeded a certain percent of the time—so he made sure he made enough calls for that percentage to keep him in clover."

"That would explain his simulation," Paula said. "Mort has a tried-and-true way of dealing with a sales call, and his way just didn't fit in with the simulation situation."

"Fit!" Seeing Paula's alarmed look, Jimmy added, "Don't worry, I'm not having one. What I mean is that Mort is too smart to depend only on a high volume of calls to keep his numbers up. We've got all kinds of evidence that he concentrated on clients who would be responsive to his type of selling."

"That's true," Fred said, rechecking his notes. "He was motivated to work with—and help out—less knowledgeable prospects, such as a young contractor, a financially naive writer, and people just starting in the workforce. But when he dealt with sophisticated executives, he had trouble empathizing with their needs, so he failed to show how he could satisfy those needs. The result—no sale."

"And then, when that happened, he walked away," Jimmy added. "A busy executive put him off, so he 'cut his losses' by abandoning the effort. After messing up when he tried to sell a group policy, he decided never to try to sell that product again."

"All of which corresponds with Mort's performance in the simulation," Paula pointed out. "When his pitch didn't work on a client, he pretty much gave up, and turned his attentions to clients likely to be more responsive to his standard approach."

"That's quite revealing," Fred said. "The simulation was aimed at a sales situation common to those encountered by UnitedCo's salespeople—and Mort was clearly lacking. But it also gives insight on two other dimensions."

"Motivational Fit, for one," Jimmy said. "Mort is a hard worker, likes to sell, and is motivated to make sales. But he's not motivated to sell your product to your kind of client."

"The other would be Resilience," Fred suggested. "Avoiding certain sales situations is not Resilience. A resilient person keeps trying to improve after rejection and is eager to try out new skills—not to avoid similar rejection."

Fred looked on as Jimmy, with Paula's agreement, amended downward Mort's ratings in the three dimensions. Yet while Fred could see how the integration of data had told them something important, the big picture still eluded him.

CHAPTER TWENTY-NINE

Fred reported that Jennifer had done superbly on the simulation. Indeed, her performance was so strong that they agreed to raise her rating in Sales Ability to a 5. "I honestly can't see a weakness that would suggest she isn't nearly the ideal candidate," Fred said.

"I'd like to take another look at Judgment," Paula said. "I'm troubled by the STAR where she left her library check-out desk and the one where her pager failed."

"I see positive aspects to those two instances," Fred said. "In the first she covered two positions, with the minor downside that patrons had to wait a minute or two before

◄

checking out books. In the second she realized that even though she could reasonably take Fridays off, she might need to be contacted, and took adequate steps."

Paula asked Fred, "As a manager, how would you feel if one of your salespeople lost a sale because she was out of touch?"

"Disgruntled," Fred said. "I give you that point. It's reasonable to expect that she would have organized some form of backup."

"It's possible that because Jennifer is genuinely strong in Analysis, we made the mistake of assuming that good judgment went along with it," Paula said. "Could it be that Jennifer's poor judgments are actually tied to her independent streak?"

Paula's choice of words triggered another brainstorm for Jimmy. "She's independent, all right," he said. "I noticed that when she spoke of the organization, it was always 'I' and never 'we.' On three occasions she even referred to the product as 'my software.'"

"I obtained a STAR that speaks to that," Fred said. "A client had a disagreement with a technical person over program customization. Jennifer took the client's side and had the techie removed from the job. But the techie was correct, and the client lost money. Jennifer's knee-jerk response to what she believed would please the client was a judgmental mistake."

"Listen to this." Jimmy found the STAR he was looking for. "I asked her how she follows up her sales—and she said she doesn't! She sees herself on the front line, and her job is to sell. After that, the technical support people take over. She doesn't contact a client again for a year, when it's time to sell them an upgrade. I didn't get any sense of integration of effort between the technical people and Jennifer."

"And while she said she liked a team approach, she doesn't even enjoy playing doubles tennis," Fred noted. "That seems contradictory."

"It fits with some data I obtained concerning Jennifer's reasons for leaving her present job," Paula noted. "She said she was seeking an opportunity to pursue sales with less dependence on factors that she has no control over."

Jimmy considered. "Remember how I speculated that her assertiveness was positive, since it came from the desire to prove herself despite her disability? I think I was wrong and right at the same time."

Fred was perplexed. "How's that?"

"Jennifer is motivated to make the big sale, all right," Jimmy said. "However, from what we've learned, that motivation gets in the way of ongoing customer service and being a team member."

"And those are key factors at UnitedCo," Fred added.

Paula went to the chart. "Should we reconsider our ratings in Judgment and Motivation?"

They did, lowering each from a 4 to a 2. Fred felt more disappointment than he had with Mort. Jennifer was a better candidate, but Fred could see now that she was not the likely successful candidate for him.

Fred's only consolation was that Paula seemed unbowed. Hoping her confidence reflected ultimate results, Fred took a deep breath as they redirected their attention to Millicent.

CHAPTER THIRTY

Jimmy helped himself to a second piece of zucchini bread. "All along, Millicent has been near the top of my list for The Faker," he said. "Now, when you look at her ratings, they seem to back up my suspicions— yet at the same time, they don't."

"She's more than satisfactory in six of our nine dimensions," Fred amplified, "yet she falls short in two of the most important, Sales Ability and Motivation."

"Let's reexamine those," Paula said. "How did she do in the simulation, Fred?"

"She was very good, though not perfect," Fred recalled. "She clarified the situation and the customer's major concerns, explored their implications, and responded with compelling features of the product she was selling. I felt that she was trying to be helpful, and when I presented the scripted objections, she showed why they didn't apply or were unimportant. However, I think she started talking about the product too soon."

"How so?" Paula asked.

"Well," Fred continued, "after she understood the problems and their implications, she should have checked with me about what kind of solutions would be appropriate and what the value of those solutions would be."

"I'm not sure I follow you," Paula said.

"Let me give you an example," Fred offered. "When I said that customer satisfaction levels were low and that was having negative impacts on our market share and sales force morale, she might have asked if I saw the solution in improving my staff's customer service skills, or in improving the quality of our products—or both. In other words Millicent did recognize my needs in general, but she failed to clarify those needs. By not learning that I wanted to improve product quality, she didn't have all the necessary information for focusing her product discussion."

"That makes sense, though," Jimmy said. "All along, I had trouble seeing how we could consider someone who has never sold."

Fred had a thought. "She's answered that all along," he said, "but it took her strong performance in the simulation to make it clear to me. The fact is, she has sold. She sold the senior citizens on the real estate tax increase, she persuaded the downtown merchants to accept parking meters, she showed the board of the Waterfront District Renewal Project how converting an old pool hall into a day care center would help attract community support, and she even sold her husband on the advantages of her returning to work."

"So she does understand the importance of customer needs," Paula agreed, "as she demonstrated in the simulation—and she also demonstrated the behaviors you're seeking."

"Exactly," Fred said. "She just needs to take it one step further by asking more questions to further pin down the situation so she can meld the answers into her discussion of how her product is the solution."

"Is this something you can help her develop through training or coaching?" Paula asked.

"Absolutely," replied Fred, "and the more I think about her performance in the simulation, along with many more examples of the type you just outlined, I feel that she's a natural. What would you think of a 4 in Sales Ability? Heck, with a bit of direction, I think she could be a 5."

"That still leaves Millicent's suspicious rating of 1 in Motivation," Jimmy insisted. "Remember, she told me flat out that she wasn't even sure if she could sell your product."

"Maybe she was wrong about that," Paula said slowly.

"Oh sure," Jimmy said sarcastically. "This system is so good it can reveal stuff about a person that she doesn't even see in herself."

"Perhaps it can," Fred said. "I think we gave Millicent a low rating because when she initially entered the hiring process, she was self-effacing. But look at how much more confident she became as we continued. Furthermore, motivations emerged from the behaviors she described that contradict her own doubts."

"She's gotten a lot of satisfaction from her experience in selling ideas," Paula agreed. "In every group she was a part of, from civic organizations to the city council, she gravitated toward the people who could influence a decision. She got satisfaction out of persuading others to go along with her ideas, and when she did, those ideas yielded positive results."

Fred shuffled through his notes until he found what he was looking for. "Millicent told me about a time she was soliciting a major contribution from a corporate foundation for the Literacy Council. She got it by promising to redirect some of the funds back into the company's high school equivalency diploma program for its workers. She was pleased, of course, but her major gratification came from how the workers and the Council both profited. That's the sort of behavior I'm looking for."

"We were kind of all wet on that 1 in Motivation," Jimmy said. "Would a 4 be more on the spot?"

The others agreed. "But darn," Jimmy said. "How could we have been so far off the mark?"

"It happens," Paula said, "and in my detecting experience, it happens all too often when we accept the superficial answers or are biased in some way by a person's background."

"But this Targeted Solution system of yours keeps us from falling into those traps," Fred said. "With three people interpreting the data, we're getting much clearer insights into what it means."

"Yeah, but there's one insight we're lacking in a big way," Jimmy said. "Why was Millicent so unforthcoming and secretive about her acting background?"

"That bothered me quite a bit, Jimmy," Fred said, "and I gave a great deal of thought to your report. Just this morning I realized that it was, in fact, an incomplete STAR."

"How so?"

"It lacked a result. Knowing she's an actress and knowing that The Faker must be a good at acting, we assumed that Millicent is a *good* actress." Fred smiled with satisfaction. "As it turns out, that isn't true."

"So you've been doing a little investigating on your own," Jimmy said.

"Call it a sort of reference check," Fred said. "I went to the library and looked up Millicent in the index of the *News-Gazette.* I found reviews of three plays she appeared in. Unfortunately, her performance in each was harshly panned."

"Three plays?" Jimmy echoed. "If the critics raked her over the coals, why did she keep going back?"

"We can only guess, but I think we can make a pretty good one," Fred suggested. "It fits well with her satisfactory rating in Resilience. After all, when you're panned but you have the intestinal fortitude to expose yourself to the same result, that's positive Resilience."

"But why wouldn't she discuss it with me?" Jimmy asked.

"Because she's human," Paula answered. "Who of us likes talking about our failures? Besides, she knew it wasn't job related. We thought it was—Good Acting Ability being a dimension for The Faker—but obviously it doesn't have anything to do with success as the Central District sales representative."

"What about my notion that acting and sales have points in common?" Jimmy asked.

"That's only superficially true," Fred said. "An actor 'sells' himself as someone else, while the effective salespeople that I've known get results by being themselves. At that, Millicent is excellent, as we've seen by the results of her 'sales' in her civic and charitable activities and her performance in the simulation."

"I think we can close the door on this acting issue," Paula said.

"I'm impressed," Jimmy said. "We've nailed down the true facts about Millicent. Now let's see if we can do the same for Thomas."

CHAPTER THIRTY-ONE

As predisposed as he had been to Thomas, Fred found his performance in the simulation oddly disappointing.

"In what way?" Paula asked.

"He did a good job in using the prework to prepare as far as the product went," Fred explained, "but he didn't seem to pay much attention to the information on the client. Then, in the simulation itself, I gave several clues that the client's main concern was risk. Thomas missed those hints, even though I made them increasingly obvious. Instead, he assumed that the sale hinged on costs. So every time I raised one of the scripted

►

objections, his response was to cut prices. At one point when he said, 'I'm sure we can work something out,' he sounded almost conspiratorial."

"That makes sense," Jimmy said.

"Not really," Fred said. "Certainly price is a factor with any customer, but it's rarely the only one."

"I meant it makes sense compared to other stories Thomas told us," Jimmy said. "The way he made sales always seemed to deal with cost. He offered a discount to one client, a satisfaction-or-your-money-back deal to another, and for a third he broke down the bill so the POs could go though."

"Money also crops up often," Paula pointed out. "He expressed his pride in being a top salesman in terms of the free vacations he won, and the reason he worked long hours during one period was to buy a second home. And at one point he said to me, 'I'm gratified by bringing home the bacon. Let's be honest, none of us are in sales for our health.'"

"He told me that sales was like climbing a cliff," Fred added, "when you know there's a treasure chest at the top."

"So he made sales by manipulating costs and 'beating the system,'" Paula said. "But let's take another gander at Motivational Fit," she continued. "Are we sure Thomas is a team player?"

"I don't know," Fred said. "All of his examples of teamwork had to do with situations like organizing a marketing approach or hiring a new person—none had to do with selling as part of a team."

"There was a time he worked long hours so he could win a bonus," Jimmy said, "but that seems to be more about money again."

"Among the dislikes he gave me was paperwork," Paula said. "Yet we heard a number of situations where he seemed happy with that chore—as long as it didn't have to do with selling."

As the discussion continued, Fred was dispirited to see Thomas' ratings dropping. In Planning and Organizing a similar pattern emerged: The STARs did not directly address strategizing relative to making sales. That also seemed to be the case in Judgment, as shown in an example of counseling a colleague on a harassment issue. There was nothing wrong with his judgment, but it didn't much relate to sales.

"Despite the simulation, the fact of the matter is that Thomas sells," Fred said with some frustration. "Isn't that the bottom line?"

When they finished their discussion, Paula added the changes in Thomas' ratings to those she'd already made for the other three candidates.

	Mort	Jen	Milli	Thomas
Persuasiveness/ Sales Ability	~~3~~2	~~4~~5	~~2~~4	~~4~~2
Resilience	~~4~~2	4	3	~~3~~2
Analysis	3	4	4	~~4~~2
Planning and Organizing	3	3	4	~~3~~2
Judgment	3	~~4~~2	4	~~4~~3
Initiative	3	4	4	~~4~~3
Motivational Fit	~~4~~2	~~4~~2	~~1~~4	~~4~~1
Oral Communication	3	3	4	5
Impact	3	3	4	4

CHAPTER THIRTY-TWO

Paula led Fred and Jimmy down the hall. At its end she opened an ornate door. "Come into my thinking chamber," Paula said mysteriously.

This den, windowless and dimly lit, contained a desk, settee, and two swivel chairs facing the wall. On the mantelpiece of the fireplace sat a foot-high, enameled statue of a black bird.

Awestruck, Jimmy touched the replica of the Maltese Falcon. "The stuff that dreams are made of," he said in his best Humphrey Bogart imitation.

Thinking of Sam Spade reminded him of something. "Hold on," he said suddenly.

►

"There's still one part of the mystery we haven't solved. Who wrote that anonymous letter?"

Paula addressed the back of one of the swivel chairs and said, "Would you care to comment on that?"

The chair slowly turned, revealing a shadowy figure.

"I presume," the figure said suavely, "that you are about to suggest that I did."

The figure rose and loomed menacingly. Jimmy reached inside his trench coat for his gun—until he remembered he didn't own a gun.

The figure advanced into the light—and they saw it was The Boss.

The Boss turned to Paula. "If you plan to accuse me of engineering something nefarious," he said pleasantly, "you'd better have proof."

Paula smiled. "I suspected you from the beginning," she said. "There are many detectives in The City, and I thought it a coincidence that Fred happened to approach the one who'd handled a previous case for you."

"The month-old newspaper on your desk, Fred!" Jimmy exclaimed. "You found it right after The Boss left your office—conveniently displaying the article about Paula."

"From the prior case I handled for you, I also knew something about how you like to operate," Paula continued to The Boss. "You have a flair for the melodramatic, having acted with The City Amateur Theater League for many years. You enjoy intrigue of the harmless sort. Perhaps the most important dimension, in which you rate quite highly, is avoidance of preaching to your department heads in favor of guiding them to discover solutions on their own."

"Circumstantial evidence," The Boss protested.

"Then let me add some hard facts," Paula pressed on. "While your secretary was at lunch, I pilfered some magazines from your reception room—the ones you used to clip the words and letters to compose your missive. It was on the type of bond paper that UnitedCo uses, and it was pasted up with 7/8-inch tape. According to City Office Supply, yours is the only company that orders that width in bulk."

Paula opened a desk drawer and extracted a paper. Jimmy saw that it was the letter of agreement that Paula had dictated to The Boss. "This was the clincher," Paula said.

Over Paula's shoulder, Jimmy read the opening sentence of the handwritten memorandum: "I hereby emploi Paula Pointer . . ."

"Jumping Jahoosis Jehosephat!" Jimmy yelped. "Where's that anonymous letter?" Paula gave it to him. "'Emploi,'" Jimmy said. "It's misspelled the same way in both!"

"You've got me dead to rights," The Boss confessed.

Jimmy turned to Paula. "Wait a goldarned second. If you knew all along that The Boss was behind this scheme, why did you go along with it?"

"You provided the clue that pointed to that," Paula said, "when you gave me the notion that The Faker must have a motive beyond pure fakery."

"I did?" Jimmy gulped.

"There had to be a purpose behind all of this, and I didn't know why The Boss cooked it up," Paula said. "From professional pride, I wanted to find out—and to discover The Faker according to the terms of The Boss' game. Besides, there was a possibility that The Boss didn't know which candidate The Faker was—although now I'm beginning to think he did."

"But why this elaborate subterfuge, Boss?" Fred felt a bit hurt at The Boss' ruse.

"I've got to hand it to you, Boss," Paula said. "All along you knew something I didn't. You were familiar with my methods. You knew I solved my cases based on how suspects had acted in the past, and you knew I obtained this information because I'm a pretty effective interviewer."

"I get it," Jimmy said. "The Boss figured out that the same methods would work in finding an excellent candidate, and he rigged it so that Fred, by joining our investigation, would learn Paula's system."

"It's just as you said, Paula," Fred amplified. "Your job was to determine who *dunnit*, and mine to determine who *will* do it—and the best way to go about our twin tasks was quite similar."

"Exactly," The Boss said. "Now then—did my little plan work?"

"It certainly did," Fred said. "It worked so well that I'm going to adopt your system for hiring from now on, Paula. If you don't mind a bit of a play on Jimmy's phrase, I'll call it Targeted Selection®."

"Then you've found a salesperson who is predicted to succeed?" The Boss asked.

"We found three," Jimmy said. "But only one of them is targeted to succeed for UnitedCo."

Jimmy took a moment to savor The Boss' suspense, then went on to explain that both Mort and Jennifer *were* in fact effective salespeople. Jimmy briefly reviewed the evidence they'd dug up. In its consistency it revealed that neither was The Faker—and that neither was right for UnitedCo.

"Then that means either Millicent or Thomas is The Faker." The Boss smiled pleasantly. "Do I have to guess?"

"No," Paula said.

She turned to the other swivel chair. "It's time to face the music."

Paula paused dramatically, then said, "Show yourself, Thomas Goldman."

CHAPTER THIRTY-THREE

Thomas was indeed the occupant of the chair, and as he rose from it, he asked, "Where did I go wrong?"

"Everywhere," Jimmy snapped.

Fred stepped in. "Your behaviors, Thomas," he said. "They just weren't those of a salesperson. Take your supposed Sales Ability. When asked about the 'one that got away,' you had only one example—and that one 'wasn't your fault.' But everyone fails now and then, and those experiences stick with you. They might not bring you down if you're resilient, but you sure as heck don't forget about them."

◄

Fred turned on his heel. "Yet you had many successes— some of them rather grandiose. You claimed three major sales of sophisticated products 'on the spot.' In all my years in sales, I've never seen that happen. You either had to be the greatest salesman in history—or a liar."

"And the latter was much more likely given your purported behaviors in other dimensions," Paula picked up. "You detailed fine performance in Analysis, Planning and Organizing, Initiative, and Judgment—but always with regard to managerial duties, and never involving actually selling a product."

"I told you what you wanted to hear," Thomas protested.

"No, you didn't," Jimmy said. "You told us what you *thought* we wanted to hear—and it wasn't what a real salesman would say."

"You assumed that money was the main motivator, for both seller and buyer," Fred said. "But money is often well down the line of motivators. Any experienced salesperson learns that early in a career."

"You thought making the sale was the sole objective," Paula pressed. "You paid little attention to customer needs or satisfaction."

Thomas shook his head. "You three are good."

"We're not finished, buster," Jimmy said. "Your answers had no consistency. You claimed to like teamwork, yet you never talked about working with people in a team.

You analyzed clients by reading corporate and technical reports, but you didn't delve any deeper. Your idea of record keeping was throwing everything about a client into a manila folder, which you consulted now and then."

"In sum," Fred added, "your behaviors, as you reported them, were simply not the credible behaviors of a successful salesperson."

"And here's the clincher," Jimmy accused. "That business about sales being like climbing to a treasure."

"What about it?" Thomas said mildly.

"It's a line from a play I saw the other night," Jimmy said. "It was called *Demise of a Sales Rep*."

"I saw that play as well," Thomas admitted. "I guess the line stuck in my mind."

"Now it's time for your demise, you faker." Jimmy turned to Paula. "Shall I cuff him?"

"Let's not get carried away," The Boss said hastily.

Jimmy decided to hear him out. Besides, he remembered that he didn't own any handcuffs either.

"Thomas is UnitedCo's new director of Human Resources," The Boss continued. "When he came on board, naturally we had several detailed discussions about the selection system we use at UnitedCo, and your loss of Central District sales reps came up, Fred. I explained that otherwise you were a fine manager and that I wanted to see you succeed."

"So that's why you were hanging out in the Human Resources office playing Gobble-Gal when Fred encountered you there," Jimmy said.

"Actually, I was reviewing some employee evaluations," Thomas said. "However, anticipating that I might be caught in an apparently suspicious situation, I worked up my alibi in advance, and programmed a 'hot key' on the computer that would instantly save the file and bring up Gobble-Gal. I hit it as soon as Fred entered."

"That's pretty smart thinking," Jimmy admitted.

"Thank you," Thomas smiled. "But to get back to my story, I suggested that I go through the hiring process to see if I could identify the mistakes you might be making, Fred."

"That gave me my idea," The Boss added. "At the same time Thomas was going through the hiring process, I decided it was a good opportunity to train you in Paula's system."

The Boss smiled again. "From what you've told me about Millicent and her chances of success, I'd say my machinations have paid dividends."

"I guess that's true," Jimmy said grudgingly. "Millicent is going to stick to UnitedCo like glue and make everyone plenty of dough. I'll bet you a two-spot on that."

"No bet, Jimmy," The Boss said. "If I took you up on it, I'm sure I would be down a two-spot."

CHAPTER THIRTY-FOUR

Fred visited Paula's office a few months later. Jimmy now had his own desk, where he sat dressed in a sport coat, slacks, and a tie. "What happened to your slouch hat, trench coat, and wing tips?" Fred inquired.

"I decided I was dressing old-fashioned," Jimmy said, "the same way I was trying to be a detective. You know, Fred, after we solved your mystery, I realized that going about my business on the basis of what I'd seen others do and using bits and pieces of methods I figured would work because people had always used them wasn't the way to nail my culprits."

"And you *have* been nailing your culprits lately," Paula said supportively. "How about you, Fred?" She smiled. "Did you find your 'culprit'?"

"I did," Fred said enthusiastically. "It looks like Millicent is going to exceed Joe Jackson's average billings in her very first quarter. She fits in well with our organization, and I'm sure as heck happy with her performance—and so is The Boss."

Fred took a pamphlet from his briefcase. "Thomas Goldman was so impressed with our results in 'fingering' both him and Millicent that he asked me to design this manual highlighting the components of your system. He also borrowed me to conduct a training session in Targeted Selection for his human resource people— they're training all the managers in the company, and it's working extremely well."

Fred proudly held up a shiny new computer disk, "Our Systems people have developed computer software that does a Job Analysis to define the dimensions for a job and prepares an interview guide for each interviewer. Do you remember how much time that took us?"

Fred gave Paula a copy of the manual and disk. "I'm sure this will be useful to both Jimmy and me," she said.

As Fred left them, Jimmy started to rise from his chair to look at Fred's booklet—and stopped short.

For the first time since he hired on with the detective agency, Paula had called him "Jimmy" instead of "Kid."

"I'll be a horse-swaggled hog-nosed horny toad," Jimmy swore.

Paula shook her head wearily. "You've still got a mouth on you," she observed. "At least some things don't change."

★ ★ ★

A REFERENCE GUIDE
TO TARGETED SELECTION®

Introduction:

The selection of a new employee is a major investment for both your organization and the candidate. Promoting a totally qualified person is even more important. Developing and maintaining a selection system that yields solid returns—productive employees and leaders who enjoy their responsibilities and seek opportunities to continuously improve their jobs—is critical to the success of every organization.

An effective selection system shares three goals:

1. **Accuracy** is the ability of your selection process to validly predict candidates' job performance.

2. **Equity** is the assurance that your selection system gives every qualified applicant a fair and equal chance to be selected.

3. **Buy-in** is the extent to which every person involved in the selection process perceives that it is worthwhile and effective, that it is beneficial to all parties regardless of the ultimate hiring decision, and that it maintains the image of the organization and the dignity of all candidates.

The Targeted Selection methodology presented in this book is a proven, practical, consistent, legally credible system that provides a firm foundation for accurate hiring decisions and provides the tools and skills to gather and

evaluate data effectively. Development Dimensions
International developed Targeted Selection in 1972, and
today it is used by more than 2,500 organizations around
the world. Its validity has been proven by numerous
research studies showing decreases in employee turnover
and accidents and increases in productivity, sales, and job
performance.

Targeted Selection was developed to overcome the most
common interview problems defined through academic
research and in thousands of selection and promotion
interviews observed by Development Dimensions
International consultants. The following pages contain
the common interview problems identified in the research
and illustrated in the story by some of Fred's and Jimmy's
early mistakes. Following each presentation of common
problems is the solution that Targeted Selection
methodology provides. Finally, we point out how using
the Targeted Selection methodology brought the three
detectives closer to solving the case.

Common Problem #1: **Interviewers involved in selection fail to seek applicant information on the dimensions necessary for success in the job and overlook important information.**

- Managers selecting individuals for the same position depend on varying and conflicting lists of dimensions and differ on the importance assigned to them.

- Gathering non-job-related information is illegal in the United States and many other countries.

TARGETED SELECTION
SOLUTION #1:
IDENTIFY THE CRITICAL JOB
REQUIREMENTS (TARGET
DIMENSIONS) FOR THE
POSITION.

Meeting with Joe Jackson, Fred discovered that Joe had many strengths—but they were not the strengths required of the sales representative that Fred must employ. Later, Jimmy asked Jennifer questions that were illegal—and equally important, of no help in a search for the most qualified candidate because they were not job related.

To focus their interviews, the three detectives decided to target the dimensions relevant to sales. They came to understand that there are three kinds of dimensions— involving knowledge, motivation, and behavior. To select the dimensions on which to focus their investigation, they met some UnitedCo salespeople who had demonstrated success in sales and sales managers who had observed successful and unsuccessful salespeople. From this information they defined the dimensions of the job and developed lists of key behavioral actions related to success in the dimensions.

Common Problem #2: Interviewers ignore job motivation and organizational fit.

- "Can do" does not equal "will do." A manager must seek people who are motivated to do the particular work of a particular job.

- Failure to determine motivation leads to poor performance and early turnover.

- Companies differ in methods of operation and their vision and values. When a company does not consider organizational fit, new hires can end up dissatisfied and frustrated.

TARGETED SELECTION
SOLUTION #2:
OBTAIN AND EVALUATE
DATA ON JOB MOTIVATION
AND ORGANIZATIONAL FIT.

Early in the course of the investigation, Joe Jackson revealed to the detectives that he was highly motivated to learn about UnitedCo products and to help customers make the best use of those products. Originally, when Fred hired Joe, he interpreted this to mean that Joe was motivated to sell those products; in fact, Joe was more motivated to work with the client in using the product. Joe's leaving was a simple matter of likes and dislikes.

But the detectives came to realize that motivation does not exist in a vacuum. An effective selection system delves into an individual's motivation as it specifically applies to a particular job and the organization in which the job is performed.

Two subsets of Motivational Fit are important to success in a job: (1) fit to the required tasks and (2) fit to the vision and values of the organization.

In the novel the trio reduced Jennifer's rating on Motivational Fit from 4 to 2 with regard to both of these criteria. First, her personal needs were addressed by making the "big kill"; however, UnitedCo depended on personal attention to clients, regardless of the size of the account, and assiduous follow-up. Second, Jennifer demonstrably was not a team player, while UnitedCo sold complicated products that required team selling and emphasized partnering with clients.

Jennifer was an excellent salesperson, but she was not Fred's qualified candidate. It was critical that the new sales representative's motivations fit into UnitedCo's evolving team strategy—and that did not describe Jennifer.

Common Problem #3: Interviewers misinterpret applicant information.

- Interviewers "play psychologist."

- Interviewers ask theoretical questions about what the applicant *would* do, not what the applicant *has done*.

- Interviewers fail to pin down sufficient details to understand the behavior completely.

TARGETED SELECTION
SOLUTION #3:
USE PAST BEHAVIOR
TO PREDICT FUTURE
BEHAVIOR.

When interviewing Mort, Jimmy asked a theoretical question and a leading question. Soon afterward, Fred helped Jimmy to get the complete story of Dukes Finnegan's fight with The Champ.

From this encounter the detectives learned that theoretical or incomplete information leads to misinterpretation. To solve this problem, Fred came up with his brainstorm of the STAR mnemonic (Situation,

Task, Action, Result). Having come to the logical conclusion that we all routinely use past behavior to predict future behavior, they could see that Fred's STAR acronym would be a great help in obtaining complete behavioral data that could be evaluated accurately without guesswork or unhelpful attempts at amateur psychology.

Common Problem #4: Interviewers overlap in their coverage of some dimensions.

- When interviewers ask similar questions, they must make judgments based on the same limited information.

- While overlap provides a check on reliability, it should be minimized to allow full coverage of all dimensions and of each dimension in greater depth.

Common Problem #5: Managers ask illegal, non-job-related questions.

- Such questions expose an organization to legal action.

- Such questions are not behavioral and do not address dimensions.

- Candidates are not treated fairly and equally.

Common Problem #6: Managers have not organized the various selection elements into a system.

- Time is wasted on applicants who should have been screened out.

- Applicants are not processed systematically, and decision points are not clearly defined.

- All applicants are not treated the same, resulting in unfairness and the risk of legal problems.

Common Problem #7: Interviewers make "snap" decisions about applicants, which affect the subsequent course of questioning.

- Interviewers decide the merits of an applicant on initial and often trivial information.

- Interviewers do not seek additional facts, which results in decreased accuracy.

TARGETED SELECTION
SOLUTION #4:
ORGANIZE DATA GATHERING
INTO A COMPREHENSIVE
DIMENSION-BASED
SYSTEM.

Faced with the challenges of "unmasking" both The Faker and a candidate who would succeed as a UnitedCo salesperson, Fred and Jimmy stumbled at several junctures. Because he arrived after Fred interviewed Joe Jackson, Jimmy was unaware of what already had been discussed, so he repeated many of Fred's questions, which Joe found annoying.

For his part Fred recognized that, in the past, he had treated candidates unequally by asking other managers to interview some but not all of them. Both he and Jimmy were prone to snap judgments: Fred had given weight to a firm handshake, while Jimmy, in his eagerness, offered solutions to the twin mysteries before all "the evidence" (the behavioral data) had been gathered.

To address these miscues, the detectives devised a selection system. Each would interview all of the candidates, "divvying up" the dimensions so all would be covered by at least two of the three interviewers. To avoid overlap, they developed interview guides containing unique, well-thought-out, behavioral questions that were legal, job related, and designed to elicit complete STARs in each dimension.

This component of the Targeted Selection system encouraged them to withhold decision making until they obtained all data. Even with complete STARs, they understood that they must save and then compare and contrast their data through a systematic integration process.

The novel also alludes to the other elements of a selection system, including recruiting, resume screening, "knock-out data" (such as a candidate for a clerical position who does not possess keyboarding skills), preliminary interviewing by Personnel, reference checks, and a physical exam (which may be required only after the job offer). When organized around dimensions, all the steps in the selection system are job related, and the system is applied consistently for all candidates.

Common Problem #8: Applicants are turned off by the interviewing process.

- Treatment that damages people's pride creates a negative atmosphere.

- When an interviewer allows interruptions or talks more than the interviewee, it implies a lack of interest.

- Candidates who are not given the opportunity to ask questions leave with a poor understanding of the job and with the impression that the organization doesn't care about their needs.

Common Problem #9: Interviewers take insufficient notes.

- Incomplete documentation of interviews discriminates in favor of applicants who make the strongest "impressions."

- Without sufficient notes managers depend on "gut feelings" or cluster their ratings in the middle of a rating scale.

- Taking notes only about negative information sends an off-putting message to the interviewee.

TARGETED SELECTION
SOLUTION #5:
APPLY EFFECTIVE
INTERVIEWING SKILLS
AND TECHNIQUES.

Hearing how Jimmy had interrupted his interview with Millicent to check on a bet, Fred recalled that he'd treated candidates similarly. Subsequently, Fred became much more careful to maintain candidates' self-esteem by establishing a friendly, professional interview atmosphere and by complimenting candidates when their achievements were genuine. Fred could see that an interview should be a fulfilling experience for both parties, and to make it so, the candidate must be put at ease, must feel good about his or her performance in the interview, and should feel that the interviewer is placing negative STARs in the proper perspective.

For his part Jimmy learned that "third degree" interrogation tactics were unproductive.

Because notes are important in recording what a candidate said, rather than what an interviewer later *thinks* was said, the detectives refined their note-taking skills.

They developed efficient methods that avoided interrupting the interview's flow, and they refrained from immediately making notes on negative data, another technique for maintaining self-esteem.

This documentation paid off later in the data integration session. Without notes on the behaviors the candidate described, the detectives would have had a difficult time defending their ratings.

Common Problem #10: Managers rely too heavily on interviews.

- Simulations provide an opportunity for the direct observation of skills.

- When applicants have little experience in the work area, relevant simulations help interviewers obtain examples of past behavior.

- Appropriate simulations pay dividends in selection accuracy because they add behavioral data about applicants.

TARGETED SELECTION
SOLUTION #6:
SUPPLEMENT INTERVIEW
INFORMATION WITH
OBSERVATIONS FROM
BEHAVIORAL
SIMULATIONS.

While Jimmy, drawing on his passion for detective novels, came up with the idea of adding a simulation to the Targeted Solution system, Paula was already aware of the usefulness of this component. In an actual hiring process, the simulation data would have been discussed along with each candidate's interview data.

The simulations provided key information that led the detectives to the twin solutions. Note that the simulation was carefully devised and consistently applied to ensure that it was relevant to the position and fair to all candidates.

Common Problem #11: Information on applicants is not integrated or discussed in a systematic manner.

- Interviewers make little attempt to systematically compare and contrast the obtained information.

- Interviewers do not discover relationships among critical information and gaps therein.

Common Problem #12: Managers' judgments are influenced by the relative quality of the applicants and by pressure to fill the position.

- Interviewers rate an average applicant more favorably than they might if there are few qualified candidates. Managers accept the "best of a bad lot" rather than continuing the search for a truly qualified applicant.

- Managers lower their standards when under pressure to hire.

Common Problem #13: Interviewers permit one dimension, favorable or unfavorable, to influence their judgment on other dimensions, or they allow their judgments to be affected by biases and stereotypes.

- The "halo effect" causes one outstanding dimension to obscure less attractive dimensions.

- Conversely, interviewers form a negative overall opinion based on mediocre behavior in a single dimension. This causes them to seek negative information and disregard positive information.

- Interviewers classify people by stereotype (for example, the "typical salesperson") and are unaware of how these prejudicial tendencies adversely affect personnel decisions.

TARGETED SELECTION
SOLUTION #7:
INVOLVE SEVERAL
INTERVIEWERS
IN ORGANIZED
DATA-EXCHANGE
DISCUSSIONS.

Data integration is the heart of Targeted Selection, and it provides the solution to the mystery of employee selection. Having obtained behavioral data objectively and in a way that was fair to all candidates, the detectives evaluated that data in a way that was equally fair and objective.

Using their system, the trio discovered that a consensus rating on dimensions cannot be a matter of "averaging" or "gut feelings." Data integration prevented them from being overly influenced by an applicant's appearance or seemingly outstanding achievements, such as sales records. They had to "put their heads together" to share the data each obtained, evaluate the insights provided, and come to a quality decision. They had to "sell" their ratings to each other by presenting supporting behavioral evidence in the form of STARs.

Data integration yielded the predicted results. Thomas Goldman's "glowing" sales record was revealed to be full of holes, while Millicent, an apparent sales neophyte, was predicted to be the candidate for whom Fred was searching.

And Millicent fulfilled the prediction.

Legal Issues in Selection

The United States Equal Employment Opportunities Commission, the Canadian government, and various city and state (provincial) equal employment commissions have issued guidelines on employment interviewing and illegal interviewing practices that result from legislation protecting certain classes, such as women, African-Americans, and the disabled. This book does not purport to cover all the issues in these guidelines, and the reader is advised to obtain and study appropriate guidelines before conducting selection or promotion interviews.

However, we believe this book deals with the two fundamental principles of legal acceptability of selection/promotion systems: job relatedness of the questions asked and consistency in the selection system across all applicants. We have not tried to tell perspective interviewers what they cannot do; rather, we have focused on what they can do—obtain meaningful, job-related information in a systematic way.

Because of space limitations, we have not included the wording of questions and the special consideration that needs to be given to individuals with disabilities during interviews.

About Development Dimensions International

At DDI we believe the workforce is the most critical factor in achieving organizational success. For more than 25 years, we've been helping organizations select and develop empowered, high-involvement workforces.

Since being founded in 1970, DDI has served more than 16,000 clients around the world, spanning a diverse range of industries and including more than 400 of the *Fortune* 500 corporations.

We are the only major human resource provider in the world to address and fully integrate the three areas essential to successful high involvement: organizational change consulting, assessment and selection systems, and training and development programs.

DDI's corporate headquarters and distribution facilities are located in Pittsburgh, Pennsylvania. It maintains 71 offices around the world, including regional training centers in Atlanta, Chicago, Dallas, Denver, Los Angeles, New York, and San Francisco, as well as operations in Argentina, Australia, Brazil, Canada, Chile, China, Finland, France, Germany, Hong Kong, Indonesia, Japan, Korea, Peru, the Philippines, South Africa, Spain, Switzerland, and the United Kingdom. DDI's programs are available in 19 languages.

Additional Products and Services from Development Dimensions International

Targeted Selection, the DDI selection system on which this book is based, has been used by thousands of organizations to reduce turnover, cut hiring costs, and make selection decisions more accurate, fair, efficient, and legally credible.

But selecting good people is just the first step in building a successful organization. DDI also helps organizations take other steps up the ladder of excellence. We offer programs and services that help your organization:

- **Create and build teams.** The harsh reality— 6 out of every 10 teams fail. But the right preparation, training, and support will put your teams on the winning side. DDI can assess your organization's readiness for teams, help you start new teams, rescue stalled teams, or nurture existing ones. We also offer training for team members and team leaders.

- **Develop leaders.** After years of managing through close supervision and tight control, today's leaders need to offer a helping hand, instead of taking a heavy-handed approach. DDI's leadership programs target all levels of leadership development—from basic day-to-day leadership skills, to high-involvement and empowering leadership skills, to executive-level skills.

- **Improve service.** With so many products and providers in the market, customers can afford to be choosy. Good service will keep them coming back again and again. DDI has programs to help your organization create a customer-focused culture, select the right people for service positions, develop customer-contact skills, and build leadership service skills.

- **Assess leadership potential.** Promoting the right people is just as important as hiring them. Accuracy of promotion decisions or the diagnosis of leadership skills for development can be enhanced by putting individuals through a series of simulations that mirror leadership situations the person will face. DDI is a pioneer in leadership assessment technology and offers a broad range of assessment programs for all employee levels.

- **Manage change.** Reengineering, downsizing, merging—these aren't just buzzwords; they're reality for thousands of organizations. DDI consultants can work with you at all stages of change—from determining whether change is needed, to deciding what form it will take, to helping you implement changes and track progress.

- **Implement continuous improvement.** For an organization to keep getting better, it needs people who can contribute ideas, do more with less, work in teams, and be involved. DDI training systems help people understand these concepts and develop the skills needed to continuously improve on the job.

- **Manage performance.** Forget the old notion that performance management is a once-a-year, one-way review. A good performance management system links people's day-to-day work directly to big-picture organizational objectives and puts people in charge of their own success. DDI has systems for both individuals and teams.

For more information about the programs and services available from Development Dimensions International, call our Marketing Information Center between 7:30 a.m. and 5:30 p.m. EST at 1-800-933-4463 in the U.S. or 1-800-668-7971 in Canada.

Also, we'd love to hear from you about your reactions to *The Selection Solution.* Send your comments to William C. Byham, President/CEO, Development Dimensions International, World Headquarters—Pittsburgh, 1225 Washington Pike, Bridgeville, PA 15017-2838, or to one of the following e-mail addresses: Internet Web Site at info@ddiworld.com or the Microsoft Network at ddi@msn.com.

Acknowledgments

Writing and producing *The Selection Solution* truly was a team effort because all aspects of the book's production, printing, and distribution were handled by DDI associates.

Many people contributed ideas, critiqued various drafts, and provided encouragement along the way. I deeply appreciate their interest, support, and involvement. DDI associates who deserve special recognition for bringing this book through the creative, editorial, and publishing processes are:

- **Tammy Bercosky and the Word Processing team,** for typing and incorporating many changes to the book as it evolved over the past 14 months.
- **David Biber**, illustrator, who created the chapter illustrations and assisted in developing the book format.
- **Jane Burchfield**, my assistant, for her tireless effort in assisting me with incorporating many people's ideas and suggestions.
- **Andrea Garry**, associate editor, who coordinated the proofreading and production of the manuscript in its final form.
- **Richard Hunter**, graphic artist, for formatting the entire manuscript and for inputting many changes.
- **Anne Maers**, publishing/marketing consultant, who acted as team leader for this project, orchestrated everyone's involvement through each stage of production, and coordinated our distribution network and marketing.

- **Helen Moretti**, my administrative assistant, who coordinated many meetings and acted as "the hub" between me and everyone involved.
- **Karen Munch**, Graphics manager, who designed the text format and cover and assisted with illustration concepts.
- **Elesha Ruminski**, proofreader, who read the book many times and assisted in coordinating revisions.

Thank you, everyone, for your highly collaborative spirit and hard work.

Valuable early reviews and suggestions came from:

- **Joseph G. Cannen**, director, Compensation and Benefits, Blue Cross & Blue Shield of Pennsylvania.
- **Bruce Court**, vice president, Selection and Assessment Services, DDI.
- **Jim Davis**, Service Plus product manager, DDI.
- **LeRoy Engle**, quality curriculum manager, a *Fortune* 500 company.
- **Connie Hilliard**, Techniques product manager, DDI.
- **Rita Kopelman**, Human Resources, Michael Baker Corporation.
- **Avrum D. Lank**, *Milwaukee Journal Sentinel* staff.
- **Darlene Lea**, manager, Regional Consulting, DDI.
- **Karen Draut Long**, Cleveland Public Library.
- **Greg Nelson**, vice president, Health Care Group, DDI.
- **Beth O'Rourke**, regional consultant, DDI.
- **Russell D. Robinson**, manager, Sector Empowerment Initiatives, Motorola.
- **Debra Walker**, regional vice president, DDI.

About the Authors

William C. Byham, Ph.D., is president and CEO of Development Dimensions International, a leading provider of programs and services designed to help organizations identify, hire, and develop their human resources.

Dr. Byham has written numerous books and articles on methods of employee assessment and selection, including coauthoring the first book for managers that interpreted the original United States EEO laws (*The Law and Personnel Testing*, 1971) and an early book on the employment of women (*Women in the Workforce: Confrontation with Change*, 1972).

Along with the cofounder of DDI, Dr. Douglas W. Bray, who was previously the director of basic human research at AT&T, Byham has been instrumental in the increased use of job "simulations" as a means of enhancing the accuracy of hiring decisions. Much of the extensive research validating the use and effectiveness of simulations can be attributed to Drs. Byham and Bray.

In 1972 Byham developed Targeted Selection®, the most widely used interviewer training program in the world. The Targeted Selection program teaches interviewers how to make accurate hiring decisions by evaluating a person's past job behaviors (acquired through interviews) and current behaviors (observed in simulations) against the dimensions (competencies) required for success in an open position.

In addition to Byham's work to improve organizations' selection and promotion decisions, he has researched and written extensively on identifying "job dimensions" that relate to job success—both in the present and in the future. This fits well with another one of Byham's interests: how to develop an empowered workforce. Byham is the author of the international best-selling books *Zapp!*® *The Lightning of Empowerment* and *HeroZ*™—*Empower Yourself, Your Coworkers, Your Company.*

For the last 25 years Bill Byham has written, lectured, and consulted extensively in three major areas: (1) the improvement of employee selection and promotion decisions, (2) the use of empowerment to motivate and energize a workforce, and (3) the importance and viability of empowered work teams.

Steven M. Krauzer has authored 26 novels, including mysteries, thrillers, and westerns. A former monthly columnist for *Outside* magazine, he also has written two nonfiction books on outdoor activities, covering kayaking and winter adventures (the latter coauthored with Peter Stark). His two screenplays were produced by Roger Corman, and his novel *Dennison's War* recently was optioned for film by director Walter Hill. Krauzer is an adjunct faculty member of the English Department at the University of Montana, where he teaches creative writing. When he's not writing or teaching, Krauzer takes advantage of the opportunities for white-water rafting, kayaking, cross-country skiing, camping, hiking, mountain biking, and back-country running that abound near his home in Missoula, Montana.

Other Books by William C. Byham
and Others at DDI

Build an empowered organization:

> *Zapp! The Lightning of Empowerment* by William C.
> Byham with Jeff Cox (Also available on video and
> audio cassette.)

> *Zapp! in Education* by William C. Byham with Jeff
> Cox and Kathy Harper Shomo

> *Zapp! Empowerment in Health Care* by William C.
> Byham with Jeff Cox and Greg Nelson

> *HeroZ: Empower Yourself, Your Coworkers, Your
> Company* by William C. Byham with Jeff Cox
> (Also available on audio cassette.)

Create and sustain high-performance work teams:

> *Empowered Teams: Creating Self-Directed Work
> Groups That Improve Quality, Productivity, and
> Participation* by Richard S. Wellins, William C.
> Byham, and Jeanne M. Wilson

> *Inside Teams: How 20 World-Class Organizations Are
> Winning Through Teamwork* by Richard S. Wellins,
> William C. Byham, and George Dixon

> *The Leadership Trapeze: Strategies for Leadership in
> Team-Based Organizations* by Jeanne M. Wilson, Jill
> George, Richard S. Wellins, with William C.
> Byham

Succeeding with Teams: 101 Tips That Really Work by Richard S. Wellins, Dick Schaaf, and Kathy Harper Shomo

Team Leader's Survival Guide by Jeanne M. Wilson and Jill George

Team Member's Survival Guide by Jeanne M. Wilson and Jill George

Understand how Japanese companies operate outside Japan:

Shogun Management: How North Americans Can Thrive in Japanese Companies by William C. Byham with George Dixon

For more information write to us at Development Dimensions International, Attention: *The Selection Solution*, World Headquarters—Pittsburgh, 1225 Washington Pike, Bridgeville, PA 15017-2838; or call our Client Service Department toll free at 1-800-334-1514 between 8 a.m. and 5 p.m. EST. Be sure to request a FREE catalog of our books and book-related products.